"It's not about liberal. It's not about consul... ...nstitu-
tion. 'If it means anything to be an American citizen, it means that we cannot be locked away by our government unless we are charged with a crime,
given due process in court, and then convicted by a jury of our peers,'
Greenwald writes. Goodbye to all that—unless you and I start acting like
patriots. Reading this book—and then passing it on to a friend—is a great
way to start." —**Rick Perlstein**, author of *Before the Storm: Barry Gold-
water and the Unmaking of the American Consensus*

"Shaken from his apolitical past by George Bush's gross violations of our
cherished Constitution and the values we hold dear, Glenn Greenwald has
penned a stark account of an unaccountable administration run amok.
Often reducing complex legal issues into language anyone can understand,
Glenn shows why he's one of the smartest and most important new voices
to emerge in politics in years." —**Markos Moulitsas**, founder of Daily Kos
and co-author of *Crashing the Gate: Netroots, Grassroots, and the Rise of
People-Powered Politics*

"Each generation of Americans must learn for themselves the value and
meaning of the remarkable democracy that has been given to us by our
founding fathers. In this powerful book, Glenn Greenwald helps remind
us what has made America great and different, and provocatively challenges us to fight efforts to weaken our democracy, which has for centuries been mankind's most important and effective champion of liberty."
—**Simon Rosenberg**, president, NDN/New Politics Institute

"Glenn Greenwald's book is one of the greatest organized crime sagas ever
written. Unfortunately, the victims of this particular caper are the American people, and the mob bosses who thumb their noses at the law are the
very individuals tasked with upholding it. Greenwald's fascinating page-
turner lays bare the Bush administration's plot to scam America, and
everyone who cares about the future of democracy will find it a thor-
oughly engrossing and absorbing read. Don't plan on doing anything else
once you pick it up; you won't be able to put it down." —**Jane Hamsher**,
film producer (*Natural Born Killers*), founder of the political blog Fire-
DogLake, and author of *Killer Instinct*.

"The Bush administration has openly declared its right to violate any law or provision of the Constitution it chooses in the name of national security, nullifying the rights of citizens in the process. This is not a paranoid conspiracy theory; it is, in fact, something the administration has been surprisingly open about. Greenwald explains clearly and plainly the dangerously radical views of presidential power held by the Bush administration and how they threaten to destroy the fundamental principles on which our nation was founded. Richard Nixon once said, 'When the president does it, that means that it's not illegal.' While few have bothered to take note, the Bush administration has made this claim as well."
— **Duncan Black**, a.k.a. Atrios, founder of the political blog Eschaton

"While most of our elected officials and the national media have looked the other way, Glenn Greenwald has been doing the hard, persistent work of reporting on and analyzing the Bush administration's moves to seize unprecedented—and unconstitutional—power. No matter your political persuasion, this book is a must-read for all Americans who believe the Constitution must remain the law of this land—and a refreshing reminder that there is more than one way to be an American patriot."
— **Arianna Huffington**, editor, The Huffington Post

"Not since Nixon has America been so betrayed and attacked by an imperial presidency. Today's Woodwards and Bernsteins are citizen journalists like Glenn Greenwald, a plain-spoken patriot blowing the whistle on Emperor Bush's war on our most sacred liberties." — **John Stauber**, founder and executive director, Center for Media and Democracy, and co-author of several books, including *Weapons of Mass Deception*

"If you feel like politics don't matter, or that it makes no difference who is in control of our government, read this book! Greenwald's story, and his analysis of the national crisis we now face, serve as our wake-up call, America. It's up to each of us to heed that call—and take action. It is time to make our voices heard." — **Cecile Richards**, president, Planned Parenthood Action Fund

How Would A
PATRIOT ACT?

How Would A PATRIOT ACT?

DEFENDING AMERICAN VALUES
from a
PRESIDENT RUN AMOK

GLENN GREENWALD

WORKING ASSETS PUBLISHING
SAN FRANCISCO

EDITORIAL DIRECTOR: Jennifer Nix
EDITOR: Safir Ahmed
COPY EDITOR: Evan Camfield
PROOFREADER: Emily DeHuff
PRODUCTION CONSULTANT: Kathy Rosenbloom
DISTRIBUTION CONSULTANT: Will Rockafellow
PUBLISHING ASSOCIATE: Claudine Zap Friedberg
DESIGNERS: Miko McGinty and Rita Jules

Printed in the U.S.A.
First printing: May 2006
Printed on acid-free, recycled paper

ISBN: 0–9779440–0–X

Working Assets Publishing
101 Market Street, Suite 700
San Francisco, CA 94105

www.WorkingAssetsPublishing.com

DISTRIBUTED BY PUBLISHERS GROUP WEST

CONTENTS

Preface

I do not think much of a man who is not wiser today than he was yesterday.
—Abraham Lincoln

I never voted for George W. Bush—or for any of his political opponents.

I believed that voting was not particularly important. Our country, it seemed to me, was essentially on the right track. Whether Democrats or Republicans held the White House or the majorities in Congress made only the most marginal difference. I held views on some matters that could be defined as conservative, views on others that seemed liberal. But I firmly believed that our democratic system of government was sufficiently insulated from any real abuse, by our Constitution and by the checks and balances afforded by having three separate but equal branches of government.

My primary political belief was that both parties were plagued by extremists who were equally dangerous and destructive, but that as long as neither extreme acquired real political power, our system would function smoothly and more or less tolerably. For that reason, although I always paid attention to political debates, I was never sufficiently moved to become engaged in the electoral process. I had great faith in the stability and resilience of the constitutional republic that the founders created.

All that has changed. Completely. Over the past five years, a creeping extremism has taken hold of our federal government, and it is threatening to radically alter our system of government and who we are as a nation. This extremism is neither conservative nor liberal in nature, but is instead driven by theories of unlimited presidential power that are wholly alien, and antithetical, to the core political values that have governed this country since its founding.

And the fact that this seizure of ever-expanding presidential power is largely justified through endless, rank fear-mongering—fear of terrorists, specifically—means that not only our system of government is radically changing, but so, too, are our national character, our national identity, and what it means to be American.

Our country is at a profound crossroads. We must decide whether we want to adhere to the values and principles that have made our country free, strong, and great for the 217 years since our Constitution was ratified, or whether we will relinquish those values and fundamentally change who we are, all in the name of seeking protection from terrorism. I genuinely believe that we are extremely lucky to be the beneficiaries of a system of government that uniquely protects our individual liberties and allows us a life free of tyranny and oppression. It is incumbent upon all Americans who believe in that system, bequeathed to us by the founders, to defend it when it is under assault and in jeopardy. And today it is.

I did not arrive at these conclusions eagerly or because I was predisposed by any previous partisan viewpoint. Quite the contrary.

I first moved to Manhattan in 1991 to attend law school at New York University, and lived and worked there for the next fifteen years. Manhattan was my home and place of work on September 11, 2001. On that day, Manhattan felt like a nightmarish mix of war zone, police state, and anarchy all rolled into one. I don't know anyone whose outlook on politics wasn't altered in some meaningful way on that day. But soon we realized that our country, its institutions, and its people are strong enough to withstand any terrorist attack or any group of terrorists, and, for those who had not lost friends or family, life seemed to return to normal more quickly than anyone could have anticipated.

This is not to say that I was not angry about the attacks. I believed that Islamic extremism posed a serious threat to the country, and I wanted an aggressive response from our government. I was ready to stand behind President Bush and I wanted him to exact vengeance on the perpetrators and find ways to decrease the likelihood of future attacks. During the following two weeks, my confidence in the Bush administration grew as the president gave a series of serious, substantive, coherent, and eloquent speeches that struck the right balance between aggression and restraint. And I was fully supportive of both the president's ultimatum to the Taliban and the subsequent invasion of Afghanistan when our demands were not met. Well into 2002, the president's approval ratings remained in the high 60 percent range, or even above 70 percent, and I was among those who strongly approved of his performance.

What first began to shake my faith in the administration was its conduct in the case of Jose Padilla, a U.S. citizen arrested in May 2002 on U.S. soil and then publicly labeled "the dirty bomber." The administration claimed it could hold him indefinitely without charging him with any crime and while denying him access to counsel.

I never imagined that such a thing could happen in modern America—that a president would claim the right to order American citizens imprisoned with no charges and without the right to a trial. In China, the former Soviet Union, Iran, and countless other countries, the government can literally abduct its citizens and imprison them without a trial. But that cannot happen in the United States—at least it never could before. If it means anything to be an American citizen, it means that we cannot be locked away by our government unless we are charged with a crime, given due process in court, and then convicted by a jury of our peers.

I developed an intense interest in the Padilla case. It represented a direct challenge to my foundational political views—that we can tolerate all sorts of political disputes on a range of issues, but we cannot tolerate attacks by the government on our constitutional framework and guaranteed liberties.

My deep concerns about the Padilla case eroded but did not entirely eliminate my support for the president. The next significant item on the president's agenda was the invasion of Iraq. While the administration recited the standard and obligatory clichés about war being a last resort, by mid-2002 it appeared, at least to me, that the only unresolved issue was not whether we would invade but when the invasion would begin.

During the lead-up to the invasion, I was concerned that the hell-bent focus on invading Iraq was being driven by agendas and strategic objectives that had nothing to do with terrorism or the 9/11 attacks. The overt rationale for the invasion was exceedingly weak, particularly given that it would lead to an open-ended, incalculably costly, and intensely risky preemptive war. Around the same time, it was revealed that an invasion of Iraq and the removal of Saddam Hussein had been high on the agenda of various senior administration officials *long before September 11.*

Despite these doubts, concerns, and grounds for ambivalence, I had not abandoned my trust in the Bush administration. Between the president's performance in the wake of the 9/11 attacks, the swift removal of the Taliban in Afghanistan, and the fact that *I wanted the president to succeed,* because my loyalty is to my country and he was the leader of my country, I still gave the administration the benefit of the doubt. I believed then that the president was entitled to have his national security judgment deferred to, and to the extent that I was able to develop a definitive view, I accepted his judgment that American security really would be enhanced by the invasion of this sovereign country.

It is not desirable or fulfilling to realize that one does not trust one's own government and must disbelieve its statements, and I tried, along with scores of others, to avoid making that choice until the facts no longer permitted such logic.

Soon after our invasion of Iraq, when it became apparent that, contrary to Bush administration claims, there were no weapons of mass destruction, I began concluding, reluctantly, that the administration had veered far off course from defending the country against the threats of Muslim extremism. It appeared that in the great national unity the September 11 attacks had engendered, the administration had seen not a historically unique opportunity to renew a sense of national identity and cohesion, but instead a potent political weapon with which to impose upon our citizens a whole series of policies and programs that had nothing to do with terrorism, but that could be rationalized through an appeal to the nation's fear of further terrorist attacks.

And in the aftermath of the Iraq invasion came a whole host of revelations that took on an increasingly extremist, sinister, and decidedly un-American tenor. The United States was using torture as an interrogation tool, in contravention of legal prohibitions. We were violating international treaties we had signed, sending suspects in our custody for interrogation to the countries most skilled in human rights abuses. And as part of judicial proceedings involving Yaser Esam Hamdi, another U.S. citizen whom the Bush administration had detained with no trial and no access to counsel, George W. Bush began expressly advocating theories of executive power that were so radical that they represented the polar opposite of America's founding principles.

With all of these extremist and plainly illegal policies piling up, I sought to understand what legal and constitutional justifications the Bush administration could invoke to engage in such conduct. What I discovered, to my genuine amazement and alarm, is that these actions had their roots in sweeping, extremist theories of presidential power that many administration officials had been advocating for years before George Bush was even elected. The 9/11 attacks provided them with the opportunity to officially embrace those theories. In the aftermath of the attack, senior lawyers in the Bush Justice Department had secretly issued legal memoranda stating that the president can seize literally absolute, unchecked power in order to defend the country against terrorism. To assert, as they did, that neither Congress nor the courts can place any limits on the president's decisions is to say that the president is above the law. Once it became apparent that the administration had truly adopted these radical theories and had begun exerting these limitless, kinglike powers, I could no longer afford to ignore them.

The 9/11 attacks were not the first time our nation has had to face a new and amoral enemy. Throughout our history, we have vanquished numerous enemies at least as strong and as threatening as a group of jihadist terrorists without having the president seize the power to break the law. As a nation, we have triumphed over a series of external enemies and overcome internal struggles, and we have done so not by abandoning our core principles in the name of fear but by insisting on an adherence to our fundamental political values.

In response to the many controversies and scandals concerning its misconduct, the Bush administration has invariably dismissed them, focusing instead on deliberately spreading an all-consuming, highly exploitative fear of terrorists. No matter what the accusation, the administration trots out its favorite tool: manipulative fear-mongering. Public appearances by senior Bush officials over the last four years have rarely missed the opportunity for a calculated and cynical invocation of mushroom clouds, homicidal dictators, and a never-ending parade of new and destructive weapons. The language of fear is the Bush administration's lingo.

Upon drawing these conclusions, I developed, for the first time in my life, a sense of urgency about the need to take a stand for our country and its defining principles. I believe that the concentrated and unlimited power now claimed by President Bush constitutes a true crisis for the United States—that it has the potential to fundamentally change our national character, to irreversibly restrict our individual liberties and to radically alter our core principles. It is not hyperbole to observe that we are moving away from the founding principles of our constitutional republic towards theories of powers that the founders identified as the hallmarks of tyranny.

Despite the significance of these developments, Bush's radical theories of power have barely even been acknowledged, let alone analyzed and trumpeted, by the national media. One of the few places where any of these issues were being discussed was on the Internet, on online political web logs, or "blogs."

In October 2005, I started my own blog, and chose as its name "Unclaimed Territory"—a declaration that my particular political passion has no grounding in any partisan loyalties or ideologies. Instead, my passion emanates almost entirely from a fervent and deeply held belief in the supremacy of our constitutional principles and the corresponding duty of every American citizen to defend these liberties when they are under assault.

Although I lacked any specific plan, I created my blog with the goal of finding a way to discuss and publicize just how radical and extreme the Bush administration had become. My blog quickly grew far beyond anything I imagined, with a daily readership of 10,000 within three months.

On December 15, 2005, *The New York Times* published a journalistic bombshell when it revealed that for the last four years, the National Security Agency has been eavesdropping on American citizens in violation of the law—because it had been ordered to do so by President Bush. From the start of the NSA eavesdropping scandal, I began writing every day about what I believed were the profoundly important legal, political, and constitutional issues raised by the Bush administration's secret surveillance program.

This is not about eavesdropping. This is about whether we are a nation of laws and whether, in the name of our fear of terrorists, we will abandon the principles of government that have made our country great and strong for more than two centuries.

My blog has become one of the principal online gathering places for citizens of every ideological perspective and background who are truly alarmed by the lawbreaking powers seized by the Bush administration, and who want to take a stand in defense of the principles of government and the Constitution. Original reporting on my blog led directly to front-page news stories on the NSA scandal in media outlets such as *The Washington Post,* the *Los Angeles Times,* and Knight-Ridder. And when the Senate Judiciary Committee held a hearing on March 31, 2006, regarding Senator Russ Feingold's resolution to formally censure the president, Senator Feingold read from my blog as he questioned one of the committee's witnesses, former Nixon White House Counsel John Dean. Let it not be said that our voices cannot be heard in the halls of government.

I began my blog because I believed my country needed whatever talents or knowledge I had to offer. Our basic system of constitutional liberties is at risk. I say that because we are a country in which the president has said—expressly and repeatedly—that he has the power to act without restraints, including the power to break the law. He has not only claimed these powers but has exercised them repeatedly over the course of several years. And he still has more than two and a half years left in office.

Even when the other checks on our government fail, citizens always have the ability to take a stand for their country. For that to happen, the first requirement is that Americans be fully informed of the objective facts regarding just how radical and extreme our government has become under George W. Bush, and the sweeping, genuinely un-American powers that one man has claimed. I began my blog to provide those facts and to take a stand in defense of our nation's founding principles. That is also why I've written the book you now hold in your hands.

CHAPTER ONE

American Devolution

One Nation, Indivisible

Given how politically polarized this country has become, it is difficult even to recall the extraordinary unity we had in America in the days, weeks, and months after September 11, 2001. More than anyone else in the country, President George W. Bush was the beneficiary of that unity. All of Congress—Republican, Democrat, and independent—was lined up behind him, and a staggering 90 percent of Americans expressed approval of the president, who just ten months earlier had been elected with fewer votes than his opponent. Americans resolutely discarded their partisan differences and other long-standing divisions and stood behind their president in responding to the attack and bringing to justice the terrorists who perpetrated it.

Democrats made clear that not only would they not oppose the president, they would work vigorously with him and with all Republicans to give him all of the tools he needed to defend the nation and combat the threat of terrorism. This extraordinary bipartisan unity led, a mere three days after the attacks, to the unanimous passage by the Senate of the Authorization for the Use of Military Force (AUMF) joint resolution, which gave the president the authority to wage war, if necessary, against Afghanistan and Al Qaeda.

"This is a first step. It is the first of many," said then–Senate Majority Leader Tom Daschle of South Dakota on the day the Senate enacted the AUMF. "We want President Bush to know—we want the world to know—that he can depend on us. We may encounter differences of opinion along the way. But there is no difference in our aim. We are resolved to work together, not as Democrats or Republicans, but as Americans."

On the same day, Senator John Kerry told reporters: "The resolution we passed today leaves no doubt that the Congress is united in full support of the President. We have given the President the authority that he needs to respond to this unprecedented attack on American citizens on U.S. soil."

Senator Herb Kohl, Democrat from Wisconsin, expressed the sentiments of Democrats everywhere: "We stand together in this Chamber and with the President. Shoulder to shoulder we are prepared to do whatever is necessary to restore peace and security to the land." Wisconsin's other Democratic senator, Russ Feingold, declared after the AUMF vote: "Congress owns the war power. But by this resolution, Congress loans it to the President in this emergency. In so doing, we demonstrate our respect and confidence in both our Commander-in-Chief and our Constitution." And, on the same day, Senator Ted Kennedy, Democrat from Massachusetts, said: "I commend President Bush for his strong commitment to win the ongoing battle against terrorism, and I commend as well the strong bipartisan spirit in which Congress has joined in this all-important commitment. America will be a stronger nation because of this attack."

On September 14, George Bush made his now-famous visit to the ruins of the World Trade Center, where he put his arm around construction workers and used one of their megaphones to pledge that "the people who knocked these buildings down will hear from all of us soon." Throughout the weeks following the 9/11 attacks, while Bush made a series of public speeches, there were ongoing private meetings between the Bush administration and congressional leaders, including the Democrats who controlled the Senate, to work cooperatively in crafting legislation designed to increase the military, investigative, and law enforcement powers of the president, to enable him to apprehend the responsible parties and to prevent future attacks.

On September 20, 2001, President Bush addressed a joint session of Congress and received enthusiastic standing ovations from members of both parties. The bipartisan support for President Bush was so great that Democrats waived their right to present the traditional response to the president's address. Then–House Minority Leader Richard Gephardt of Missouri explained the Democrats' extraordinary decision this way: "I've never seen the Congress work better together in a bipartisan way. It's almost a national unity government, and that's what it should be. . . . We want enemies and the whole world and all our citizens to know that America speaks tonight with one voice."

On September 29, 2001, Al Gore delivered his first public speech since losing the 2000 election to Bush. Gore spoke at the Iowa Democratic Party's 2001 Jefferson-Jackson Day Dinner and said: "Regardless of party, regardless of ideology, regardless of religion or race or ethnicity, there are no divisions in this country where our response to the war on terrorism is concerned. We are united." He punctuated his remarks by pointedly telling his audience: "George W. Bush is my commander in chief."

And this sense of national unity was felt across the country. The president who was elected with less than 50 percent of the popular vote had sky-high approval ratings—above 70 percent all the way through August 2002, and above 60 percent through mid-2003, months after the Iraq war had started. Thus, for almost two years after 9/11, Americans in both political parties put aside their differences with the president on a whole host of political matters they judged to be of lesser importance in order to support him and his policies in the area of national security.

Illustrative of this congressional willingness to grant expansive new powers to the president was the Senate's voice-vote approval on September 13, with no hearings or debate, of a bill entitled the Combating Terrorism Act of 2001, which significantly enhanced police wiretap powers and permitted the FBI, in a wide range of circumstances, to monitor Internet communications for up to forty-eight hours without first obtaining a search warrant. Particularly in the area of investigation and surveillance, members of Congress in both parties made crystal clear that they were not just willing but eager to give the president new and sweeping powers under the law to monitor terrorists' movements and communications in order to prevent future attacks.

The breadth and strength of this unity, and the resulting acts of legislative cooperation by the Congress, reflected a climate in which George W. Bush could have asked almost anything of Congress and the American people and they would have given it to him, particularly when such requests were justified by the need to obtain greater powers to fight terrorists.

Beginning almost immediately after the September 11 attacks, the president took advantage of this congressional deference by requesting substantially more law enforcement, investigative, and surveillance powers. One of the most significant surveillance tools available to any president is the power to eavesdrop on telephone communications. The National Security Agency (NSA) has long had the technological capability to eavesdrop on every telephone conversation in the United States, a power that was of obvious importance in preventing terrorist attacks. In response to a history of abuse of this eavesdropping power by presidents of both parties from the 1950s through the 1970s, Congress enacted the Foreign Intelligence Surveillance Act (FISA) in 1978, which allowed the president to eavesdrop on both the domestic and international communications of Americans, but required that such eavesdropping be undertaken only with judicial oversight and approval.

In the aftermath of the 9/11 attacks, the White House argued that many of the FISA restrictions on the president's eavesdropping powers were too severe. It insisted that the president needed additional eavesdropping powers under the law in order to engage in effective surveillance of terrorist communications. In particular, the Bush administration requested that Congress amend several provisions of FISA so as to give the president greater flexibility and increased power to eavesdrop on all communications, including the telephone conversations of American citizens on U.S. soil.

As was true with virtually every other request made at that time by the Bush administration, both parties in Congress acceded and supported the expansion of the president's eavesdropping powers.

In October 2001, the USA PATRIOT Act was introduced. The bill, which was 326 pages long, modified numerous laws spanning a vast range of law enforcement and surveillance topics. It was principally drafted by Assistant Attorney General Viet D. Dinh and future Secretary of Homeland Security Michael Chertoff. For a bill of such complexity, size, and scope, the PATRIOT Act was drafted with extraordinary speed. A significant portion of the bill was devoted to amending FISA to give President Bush the expanded eavesdropping and other surveillance powers his administration had requested.

The PATRIOT Act and related legislation approved by Congress in late 2001 made several changes requested by the Bush administration. For instance, FISA was amended to allow the president to eavesdrop on the conversations of Americans for up to seventy-two hours—instead of the previous twenty-four—without obtaining judicial approval, whenever emergency eavesdropping was needed. It also amended FISA to allow for "roving" eavesdropping warrants, so the government could eavesdrop not only on a specific telephone number but on any and all telephone numbers used by the target of the surveillance. And FISA was amended to allow any information obtained from such eavesdropping to be shared by all intelligence and law enforcement agencies, so as to increase the ability of the government to prevent attacks.

And so, within weeks after the 9/11 attacks, Congress modernized and updated FISA to accommodate every request made by President Bush. The spirit of national unity and bipartisanship that prevailed after the 9/11 attacks thus led to one of the greatest and most rapid expansions of federal government power in our nation's history.

The PATRIOT Act was approved by the House on October 23, 2001, by the lopsided vote of 357 to 66, and in the Senate the following day by an even more lopsided 98 to 1. President Bush was quite pleased with the newly amended FISA when he signed it into law on October 26. He told the country that day that as a result of these amendments, he now had all the surveillance power he needed to track the telecommunications of the terrorists:

> Surveillance of communications is another essential tool to pursue and stop terrorists. The existing law was written in the era of rotary telephones. This new law I sign today will allow surveillance of all communications used by terrorists, including e-mails, the Internet, and cell phones. As of today, we'll be able to better meet the technological challenges posed by this proliferation of communications technology.

This is worth repeating: After Congress changed the law to conform to his requests, significantly broadening his power to eavesdrop under FISA, President Bush told the nation that he had all of the tools he needed to engage in eavesdropping to track the communications of terrorists.

The PATRIOT Act was enacted so quickly that there was virtually no time to engage in a meaningful debate before it became law. In general, I believe that whenever a country is considering a law that places increased powers in the hands of the government to engage in surveillance on its own citizens, it must do so with great caution, because there will inevitably exist a strong temptation to abuse eavesdropping powers for political and self-serving ends—a fact that has been starkly demonstrated throughout history in many different countries, including our own.

Despite those concerns, I believed then, and believe now, that it was reasonable and appropriate, in light of the terrorist attacks, to increase the president's eavesdropping powers, and therefore I favored the FISA amendments that did so. The newly amended FISA, just like the FISA which had been in place since 1978, still prohibited the president from eavesdropping on Americans without judicial oversight and approval. To me, this safeguard meant that the likelihood of abuse of these newly expanded powers was extremely low, if not nonexistent. After all, it is virtually impossible to misuse the NSA's eavesdropping powers when a federal judge on the FISA court must first authorize such eavesdropping.

The following weekend, President Bush delivered his weekly radio address and again discussed the amendments to FISA that he had just signed into law. "The new law recognizes the realities and dangers posed by the modern terrorist," he told the nation. "Under the new law officials may conduct court-ordered surveillance of all modern forms of communication used by terrorists." Bush ended the radio address by making the following pledge: "These measures were enacted with broad support in both parties. They reflect a firm resolve to uphold and respect the civil liberties guaranteed by the Constitution, while dealing swiftly and severely with terrorists. Now comes the duty of carrying them out. And I can assure all Americans that these important new statutes will be enforced to the full."

As it turns out, at virtually the same time George W. Bush was publicly pledging to the nation that he would only engage in eavesdropping sanctioned by the new law, he had secretly ordered that this very law be violated.

More than four years later, *The New York Times* revealed in a shocking story that in October 2001, at the same time that Bush was praising Congress for amending FISA to expand the eavesdropping powers at his disposal, he secretly ordered the NSA to eavesdrop on Americans *in violation of the very act that he had just signed into law.* As the December 15, 2005, story in the *Times* reported:

> President Bush secretly authorized the National Security Agency to eavesdrop on Americans and others inside the United States to search for evidence of terrorist activity without the court-approved warrants ordinarily required for domestic spying. . . .
>
> The previously undisclosed decision to permit some eavesdropping inside the country without court approval was a major shift in American intelligence-gathering practices, particularly for the National Security Agency, whose mission is to spy on communications abroad. As a result, some officials familiar with the continuing operation have questioned whether the surveillance has stretched, if not crossed, constitutional limits on legal searches.

While Congress broadened the president's eavesdropping power under FISA in October 2001, that newly amended law still made it a criminal offense to eavesdrop on Americans without judicial oversight and approval. Despite that provision, President Bush became the first president to secretly order the NSA to eavesdrop on Americans, in violation of that law.

In the four years that followed, numerous actions by the administration provoked serious concern on my part over what increasingly appeared to be an unbridled extremism and a contempt for the legal limits imposed by Congress and the courts. But the misconduct that the *Times* story revealed in December 2005 was fundamentally more alarming. This was deliberate, ongoing lawbreaking ordered personally by the president.

The picture that emerged for me in light of this *Times* report presented a sharply contradictory set of circumstances: A president who commanded the support and loyalty of national politicians in both parties. A president who sought, and was given, expanded powers by Congress to combat terrorism. A Congress that, in the aftermath of the 9/11 attacks, repeatedly and with virtual unanimity agreed to every request the president made. And yet a president who chose to secretly order eavesdropping on American citizens, on U.S. soil, in violation of the very law he had just requested.

The bipartisan support after September 11 enabled the White House—even with a Democratic majority in the Senate—to secure an unprecedentedly rapid and expansive wave of new laws increasing the powers of the president. A study by professors Margaret F. Klemm and Albert C. Ringelstein of Purdue University and Moldova State University, respectively, entitled "Congressional Response to the September 11, 2001 Terrorist Attacks," examined the September 11–related bills introduced in Congress between September 11, 2001, and June 18, 2002. In the Senate, the study found virtual unanimity across party lines on almost every issue: "Of 62 votes, 50 passed by unanimous consent or voice vote. Of the 12 roll call votes, 8 were unanimous and 3 others registered only a single dissenting vote each. The remaining vote found only 9 senators voting nay."

When George Bush ordered the secret NSA program, it was not, of course, the first time an American president had acted illegally. But what is so astounding, and so profoundly alarming, about the president's behavior is not just that he violated the law deliberately but that he did so repeatedly over the course of many years, and when he was caught he defiantly insisted that he had the right to do so, proudly vowing that he would continue to engage in warrantless eavesdropping on Americans despite the fact that the law makes it a criminal offense.

The president, who had successfully pressured *The New York Times* into withholding this story from the American people for more than a year, unabashedly proclaimed that he would continue breaking the law. It was a potent declaration that the White House believes the president's powers are so vast they entitle him even to violate the law of the land.

Listening In

Ever since World War II, the U.S. government has possessed the technological capability to eavesdrop on the private conversations of Americans, and from then until the 1978 enactment of FISA, the government, under both Democratic and Republican administrations, used that power for all kinds of legitimate—and illegitimate—reasons. During this pre-FISA period, the government intercepted communications between Soviet agents and their American collaborators. It was able to secretly record conversations involving some of the nation's most violent and dangerous criminals. But the government also eavesdropped continuously on the personal and private communications of the Reverend Martin Luther King, Jr. And it monitored the private conversations of a whole array of perceived domestic political opponents who were not even suspected of committing any crime, other than opposing the government's policies.

Monitoring the private communications of its own citizens is one of the most useful—and most dangerous—powers a government can have. If their private conversations can be intercepted, citizens have no privacy from government officials. At the same time, the government must have broad and aggressive eavesdropping powers in order to learn of the plans and actions of the country's enemies and to investigate and apprehend domestic criminals. When specific instances of eavesdropping abuses by the government first emerged in the late 1960s, America began to debate the question of how to enable the government to engage in aggressive, necessary eavesdropping while preventing it from abusing this power and listening in for its own political ends.

This danger that the government will abuse its surveillance power is not merely theoretical. American presidents of both parties—from Roosevelt to Nixon—eavesdropped in secret, with no oversight of any kind and with virtually no legal restrictions.

In 1952, President Harry S Truman issued an executive order creating the National Security Agency, to consolidate surveillance capabilities and spy on the nation's foreign enemies. But by necessity, the agency developed the technological capability to intercept the communications of American citizens on U.S. soil as well. Because of the great secrecy in which the NSA's activities were shrouded (for decades its acronym was said to stand for "No Such Agency"), it operated with virtually no legal limits or oversight of any kind. In essence, it was a secret, unaccountable agency that—despite possessing incomparably intrusive powers to intercept communications—operated under the unlimited, unchecked authority of the president.

Beginning with the Truman administration and continuing through the Eisenhower, Kennedy, Johnson, and Nixon administrations, the NSA engaged in massive and sweeping surveillance without any real restrictions or oversight.

In 1975, in response to reports of widespread eavesdropping abuses by the Nixon administration, the United States Senate created the Senate Select Committee to Study Government Operations with Respect to Intelligence Activities. The "Church Committee," named after Idaho senator Frank Church, who chaired it, was charged with investigating how presidents had used their eavesdropping powers and with determining the extent and scope of abuse. Even back in 1975, when the NSA's surveillance capabilities were primitive compared to today, Senator Church was stunned by what he learned regarding the breadth and scope of the NSA's powers. As *The New York Times* recently recounted:

> "That capability at any time could be turned around on the American people," [Church] said in 1975, "and no American would have any privacy left, such is the capability to monitor everything: telephone conversations, telegrams, it doesn't matter. There would be no place to hide." He added that if a dictator ever took over, the N.S.A. "could enable it to impose total tyranny, and there would be no way to fight back."

While that may sound hyperbolic, the potential danger of eavesdropping powers of this sort is self-evident. When the government exercised these powers in secret, abuse was rampant. According to the Electronic Privacy Information Center's January 2006 report entitled *Spotlight on Surveillance:*

> The NSA, originally created to spy on foreign enemies, began a domestic watch list program called Minaret in the 1960s. The FBI, Secret Service, the military and the CIA added names to this list of threats to national security. This list included U.S. citizens or groups involved in civil rights and anti-war activities—including civil rights leader and minister Dr. Martin Luther King, Jr. In 1975, NSA Director Lt. Gen. Lew Allen, Jr., testified before the Church committee and revealed that the NSA intercepted the phone calls of 1,200 American citizens over six years.

Isolated reports of eavesdropping abuses began, for the first time, to make Americans aware of the fact that the federal government was monitoring its own citizens. A July 25, 1969, article in *Time* magazine recounted:

> It has long been common knowledge that the government listened in regularly on the telephone conversations of Teamsters boss Jimmy Hoffa and a wide assortment of Mafia chieftains. But recently the public has also learned that the FBI indulged in eavesdropping on Negro leaders Martin Luther King Jr. and Elijah Muhammad, as well as such white radicals as David Dellinger and Jerry Rubin. Not even Capitol Hill is immune, according to Democratic Senator Ralph W. Yarborough of Texas and Republican Senator Carl T. Curtis of Nebraska, who contend that congressional telephones have also been subjected to bugging.

Ultimately, it was the government's secret, years-long monitoring of the private conversations of Martin Luther King that showed Americans just how profoundly dangerous eavesdropping can be when exercised with no oversight. The Church Committee, in its final 1976 report, detailed just how severe, invasive, and malicious had been the government's surveillance of Dr. King's communications in the previous decade—something the country had had no idea was occurring at the time:

The FBI's campaign against Dr. Martin Luther King, Jr. began in December 1963, four months after the famous civil rights March on Washington, when a nine-hour meeting was convened at FBI Head-quarters to discuss various "avenues of approach aimed at neutral-izing King as an effective Negro leader."

Following the meeting, agents in the field were instructed to "continue to gather information concerning King's personal activi-ties . . . in order that we may consider using this information at an opportune time in a counterintelligence move to discredit him."

About two weeks after that conference, FBI agents planted a microphone in Dr. King's bedroom at the Willard Hotel in Washing-ton, D.C. During the next two years, the FBI installed at least four-teen more "bugs" in Dr. King's hotel rooms across the country. Physical and photographic surveillances accompanied some of the microphone coverage.

The FBI also scrutinized Dr. King's tax returns, monitored his financial affairs, and even tried to determine whether he had a secret foreign bank account.

In late 1964, a "sterilized" tape was prepared in a manner that would prevent attribution to the FBI and was "anonymously" mailed to Dr. King just before he received the Nobel Peace Prize. Enclosed in the package with the tape was an unsigned letter which warned Dr. King, "your end is approaching . . . you are finished." The letter intimated that the tape might be publicly released, and closed with the following message:

"King, there is only one thing left for you to do. You know what it is. You have just 34 days in which to do (this exact number has been selected for a specific reason, it has definite practical significance). You are done. There is but one way out for you . . ."

Dr. King's associates have said he interpreted the message as an effort to induce him to commit suicide.

While these sorts of invasions of privacy and surveillance were, to put it mildly, clearly unethical, and while such politically motivated invasions were a distortion of the purpose of the government's eavesdropping powers, there were no laws at the time specifically barring such abuse or requiring oversight. Nor had courts yet held that the Fourth Amendment's prohibition against searches and seizures meant warrantless surveillance was unconstitutional. The government's eavesdropping on Americans was secret, and pervasive abuse was the result.

King may have been the most celebrated victim of the government's eavesdropping, but he was far from the only one. As *Washington Post* columnist Ruth Marcus summarized on January 6, 2006:

> The Church committee discovered that the NSA had for years—unbeknownst to Congress—been using a "watch list" of U.S. citizens and organizations in sorting through the foreign communications it intercepted.
>
> In addition, for three decades, from 1945 to 1975, telegraph companies had been turning over to the NSA copies of most telegrams sent from the United States to foreign countries. This program, code-named Shamrock, was, according to the Church committee report, "probably the largest governmental interception program affecting Americans ever undertaken."

The "watch list" to which Marcus refers was one of the most controversial and sweeping secret eavesdropping programs discovered by the Church Committee. Under the program known as Project MINARET, the NSA—beginning in the Johnson administration and drastically expanding its activities during the Nixon administration—had monitored the private communications of scores of American citizens, on U.S. soil, who were politically suspect in some way, typically because they belonged to civil rights or antiwar groups. Among the names on the NSA's watch list were Benjamin Spock, folk singer Joan Baez, newspaper editor David Kahn, most of the prominent protestors against the Vietnam war, and even scores of Quaker activists.

There was no possible justification for this surveillance. None of the Americans monitored by the NSA under MINARET were even suspected of committing crimes. Their communications were intercepted because they were perceived to be a political threat to the officials in power. And this abusive eavesdropping was enabled by a single fact—it occurred prior to the enactment of FISA, and therefore it was conducted without any warrant requirements and without judicial oversight of any kind. The president was free to operate in the dark, and nobody would know how the power was used other than the president's trusted underlings. Due to the deep secrecy in which so much of this presidential eavesdropping was shrouded, most of these widespread abuses did not even come to light until the sweeping investigation undertaken in the mid-1970s by the Church Committee.

While eavesdropping abuses had been going on long before Nixon arrived at the White House in 1968, their dangers first emerged as a matter of public controversy during the early stages of the Nixon administration, with the disclosure of isolated cases of abuses by the Justice Department and FBI. To assuage the public's fears, Nixon's new attorney general, John Mitchell, gave the same assurance governments always use when they want to wield new powers: There was no need to worry because eavesdropping would only be used against criminals, not ordinary law-abiding Americans. As the July 25, 1969, *Time* magazine story reported:

> During his presidential campaign, Richard Nixon said that he would take full advantage of the new law—a promise that raised fears of a massive invasion of privacy.
>
> To calm those fears, the administration last week issued what amounted to an official statement on the subject. In his first news conference since becoming the President's chief legal officer, Attorney General John N. Mitchell pointedly announced that the incidence of wiretapping by federal law enforcement agencies had gone down, not up, during the first six months of Republican rule. Mitchell refused to disclose any figures, but he indicated that the number was far lower than most people might think. "Any citizen of this United States who is not involved in some illegal activity," he added, "has nothing to fear whatsoever."

As is now known, Mitchell's assurances could not have been any less accurate. During his six years in office, President Nixon ordered the NSA to engage in a vast and sweeping program of surveillance of American citizens on U.S. soil, including many who were entirely innocent of any crimes and who were not even arguably "involved in some illegal activity." But because the surveillance was done in total secrecy, all of these abuses were concealed for years. It took an aggressive investigation by the Church Committee to discover their true nature and scope.

But long before the Church Committee, another senator helped shed light on similar abuses. Senator Sam Ervin of North Carolina was one of the most conservative Dixiecrats in the Senate—an unwavering supporter of the Vietnam War, a vigorous, even extreme, defender of free market economics, and one of the most steadfast opponents of civil rights legislation. But beginning in the late 1960s, he made it one of his top priorities to warn the nation of the dangers to core constitutional liberties and basic American principles of privacy posed by secret, unchecked governmental eavesdropping. In 1969, Christopher Pyle, a former U.S. Army Intelligence officer, revealed to Ervin's Senate Subcommittee on Constitutional Rights that the Army had been spying on ordinary American citizens who were politically suspect. At Ervin's urging, Pyle published his story in the January 1970 issue of *Washington Monthly*, in which he wrote that the Army had been spying on Americans and maintaining secret dossiers concerning "lawful political activities of civilians wholly unassociated with the military." Pyle revealed:

> Today, the Army maintains files on the membership, ideology, programs, and practices of virtually every activist political group in the country... including such nonviolent groups as the Southern Christian Leadership Conference, Clergy and Laymen United Against the War in Vietnam, the American Civil Liberties Union, Women Strike for Peace, and the National Association for the Advancement of Colored People.

Senator Ervin was determined to discover the origin and scope of this secret, unchecked Army surveillance on Americans, and he held hearings to investigate. Because the program was created by the Johnson administration, Ervin assumed that the Nixon administration would cooperate with his investigation. But he was wrong. The Nixon administration immediately began stonewalling, refusing to answer, and providing no information other than vague and uncorroborated assurances that no abuse existed outside of what it insisted were the isolated and aberrational examples Ervin had discovered. In *Senator Sam Ervin and the Army Spy Scandal of 1970–1971*, Karl Campbell recounts:

The Nixon administration's lack of cooperation troubled [Ervin], especially in light of the President's recent moves against individual rights in so many other areas. Several years later during the Watergate hearings, after listening to all the descriptions of political wiretapping and illegal surveillance, Ervin recalled his investigation of the Army's domestic spying and remembered his puzzlement at that time:

"I would expect the Republicans to be glad for the committee to bring out this evidence of how the Democratic administration permitted the Army to spy on civilians. I could not understand it. But now I do, since the revelations of these [Watergate] things were right in harmony with the spirit of these plans of 1970."

Demonstrating that the temptation to abuse secret eavesdropping powers is by no means confined to partisan affiliation or ideology, the Nixon administration picked up right where the Johnson administration left off—namely, exploiting its ability to intrude into the private communications of American citizens for its own political gain. In response to the obvious stonewalling and obfuscation which Ervin encountered in his efforts to investigate these secret spying programs, the long-serving conservative Senator, with great foresight, warned that the programs he had uncovered "appear to be part of a vast network of intelligence-oriented systems which are being developed willy-nilly throughout the land . . . [representing] a potential for political control and intimidation which is alien to a society of free men."

As a result of his discovering just how extreme these surveillance abuses had become, this conservative, prowar Southern senator—who had led the battle against the iconic liberal economic and social programs of the 1960s—became the leading defender of the liberties guaranteed to all American citizens by the Constitution, and insisted upon checks and safeguards on the government's eavesdropping powers. As part of his opening statement at the Army spy scandal hearings, Senator Ervin explained why this was a matter of such urgency: "When people fear surveillance, whether it exists or not, when they grow afraid to speak their minds and hearts freely to their government or to anyone else, then we shall cease to be a free society."

Reining in the Presidents

As a result of the numerous revelations of surveillance abuses, the country collectively decided that it could no longer entrust the federal government with the unlimited power to secretly eavesdrop on its citizens. In 1977, amid the intense controversies over abuse of power swirling out of Watergate and the Church Committee Report, both Republicans and Democrats began meeting with various executive branch officials to create a framework that would be acceptable to both political parties and that would govern how the president was permitted to eavesdrop on American citizens in the future.

Taking away the government's power to eavesdrop was not an option. The value and necessity of eavesdropping—to monitor foreign enemies and to combat domestic crime—was too great. Nobody proposed banning, or even placing substantial limits on, legitimate eavesdropping. What was needed was a mechanism, a control feature, to ensure that the government only used its eavesdropping power for legitimate purposes, not to advance the political or other self-interests of government officials by spying on innocent Americans.

The solution was the Foreign Intelligence Surveillance Act (FISA), which was approved by Congress and signed into law by President Jimmy Carter in 1978. It granted the president broad powers to eavesdrop on agents of foreign countries and terrorist groups. But it also made it a criminal offense—punishable by up to five years in prison—for any government official to eavesdrop on Americans without judicial oversight and approval. Recognizing that emergency situations sometimes require immediate eavesdropping where there is no time to obtain judicial approval, FISA allows the government to eavesdrop without such approval for up to fifteen days in times of war, and for up to twenty-four hours at all other times (a window which was increased to seventy-two hours in the aftermath of the 9/11 attacks). To provide for judicial oversight, the law created a new court, the FISA court, which—unlike any other court in the country—operated in complete secrecy, with only the government present, in order to prevent disclosure of the classified information that legitimate eavesdropping encompasses.

In light of the vastly different views in this country regarding the proper balance between liberty and security, the national consensus in favor of FISA was remarkable. It received almost unanimous support from both Republicans and Democrats in the U.S. Senate, including many Republicans, such as Senator Orrin Hatch, who continue to serve today. It was enacted with the full cooperation and agreement of the executive branch and was the by-product of substantial input from the judiciary. FISA emerged as the national consensus on how all of these competing rights, interests, and objectives should be balanced.

The national solution that grew out of these eavesdropping abuse scandals was thus grounded in one of the most fundamental principles of American government—that abuses are most effectively prevented by ensuring that all government power is subject to checks and balances, and cannot be exercised unilaterally or in secret. The debate that led to FISA was not about whether the government should have broad eavesdropping powers, but whether, in order to prevent abuse, it should be permitted to eavesdrop only with oversight. The country's enactment of FISA in 1978 represented a consensus decision that it was no longer tolerable to have elected officials eavesdrop on Americans in secret and beyond the reach of legal restrictions.

FISA remained in place through the Carter, Reagan, Bush Sr., and Clinton administrations and served the country well as America battled and then defeated the Soviet empire, fought wars in Grenada, the Persian Gulf, and Kosovo, and participated, directly and indirectly, in military conflicts against Communists around the globe. From its 1978 enactment until President Bush's 2001 decision to eavesdrop without its knowledge, the FISA court never once denied a single surveillance request by the government.

To this day, FISA continues to be the law of the land. Congress has never repealed it and no court has declared it unconstitutional. And until President Bush got caught violating the law, no administration—Republican or Democratic—had questioned its constitutionality or validity. Most important, under the law's now longstanding and widely accepted mandates, it continues to be a criminal offense in the United States for *any* government official—no matter how high—to eavesdrop on Americans without judicial oversight and approval.

The essence of FISA is that it allows the government to eavesdrop on any U.S. persons—American citizens and permanent residents—who are suspected of being either terrorists or agents of foreign states, as long as the government obtains judicial approval from the FISA court. (The government can eavesdrop on non–U.S. persons without judicial approval.) Section 1805(a) requires the FISA court to approve government requests for eavesdropping where there is probable cause to believe that the target of the surveillance is an agent of a foreign state or a terrorist group. When there is an emergency need to begin eavesdropping immediately—if, say, the U.S. military captures a terrorist and wants to begin surveillance on the telephone numbers in his cell phone before judicial approval can be obtained—Section 1805(f) of FISA allows immediate eavesdropping without a warrant for up to seventy-two hours.

Violation of FISA is a federal felony. Section 1809 thus expressly provides that a "person is guilty of an offense if he intentionally—(1) engages in electronic surveillance under color of law except as authorized by statute...." And Section 2511(2)(f) requires that FISA "shall be the exclusive means by which electronic surveillance . . . may be conducted." Section 1809(c) provides that "an offense described in this section is punishable by a fine of not more than $10,000 or imprisonment for not more than five years, or both." Thus, any government official who eavesdrops on Americans without complying with FISA's requirements for judicial oversight and approval is, by definition, committing a criminal offense.

It is worth noting that, contrary to the claims some have made, FISA is not a statute meant to apply only in peacetime. To the contrary, it was designed for eavesdropping activities in times of war as well. Section 1811 of FISA is entitled "Authorization during time of war," and it specifically provides that "the President, through the Attorney General, may authorize electronic surveillance without a court order under this subchapter to acquire foreign intelligence information for a period not to exceed fifteen calendar days following a declaration of war by the Congress."

It is clear that FISA, enacted near the peak of the Cold War against the Soviet Union, was meant to govern eavesdropping activities during war or peace. In many ways, one can legitimately argue that the time in which restrictions on the government's eavesdropping were enacted through FISA, the 1970s and 1980s, was actually one of the most dangerous periods in American history. In the year FISA was enacted, the Soviet empire had multiple nuclear warheads aimed at scores of American cities. It is difficult to imagine a circumstance in which it was more imperative for the government to be able to engage in aggressive foreign intelligence surveillance. And yet that was precisely when the country enacted FISA and required judicial oversight for its eavesdropping activities.

Now that the Soviet Union no longer exists, many have forgotten how grave a threat it posed to the United States. In a March 31, 1976, speech entitled "To Restore America," transcribed by the Ronald Reagan Legacy Project, then-presidential candidate Reagan said:

> But there is one problem which must be solved or everything else is meaningless. I am speaking of the problem of our national security. Our nation is in danger, and the danger grows greater with each passing day. Like an echo from the past, the voice of Winston Churchill's grandson was heard recently in Britain's House of Commons warning that the spread of totalitarianism threatens the world once again and the democracies are wandering without aim.

That was two years before FISA was enacted. Throughout the 1980s, as president, Reagan advocated relentlessly for a military expansion, precisely because, as he repeatedly pointed out, the United States faced one of the greatest and most formidable enemies it had ever known. Here is what he told the nation in a televised speech on March 23, 1983, when he first announced his proposal, popularly known as the "Star Wars" program, to build a space-based shield over the United States designed to repel incoming Soviet missiles:

> For 20 years the Soviet Union has been accumulating enormous military might. They didn't stop when their forces exceeded all requirements of a legitimate defensive capability. And they haven't stopped now. During the past decade and a half, the Soviets have built up a massive arsenal of new strategic nuclear weapons—weapons that can strike directly at the United States. . . .
>
> As the Soviets have increased their military power, they've been emboldened to extend that power. They're spreading their military influence in ways that can directly challenge our vital interests and those of our allies. . . .
>
> Some people may still ask: Would the Soviets ever use their formidable military power? Well, again, can we afford to believe they won't? There is Afghanistan. And in Poland, the Soviets denied the

will of the people and in so doing demonstrated to the world how their military power could also be used to intimidate. . . .

The Soviet Union is acquiring what can only be considered an offensive military force. They have continued to build far more intercontinental ballistic missiles than they could possible need simply to deter an attack. Their conventional forces are trained and equipped not so much to defend against an attack as they are to permit sudden, surprise offensives of their own.

Regardless of whether one believes that the U.S. is currently "at war," the Soviet Union was an infinitely stronger and more sophisticated enemy with far deeper resources than Al Qaeda could dream of possessing. Communists, we were always told, employed their own deadly version of "sleeper cells," systematically implanting foreign agents and even recruiting American citizens to work on their behalf, including infiltrating the highest levels of the U.S. government with their agents and sympathizers. And the United States vanquished the Soviet Union and won the Cold War without presidents Carter, Reagan, or Bush Sr. ever eavesdropping in violation of the FISA law or claiming that they had the power to do so.

Prior to the December 2005 disclosure that President Bush had violated the law, nobody had ever suggested that the FISA framework impeded necessary eavesdropping. If anything, the FISA court has long been criticized by liberals, conservatives, libertarians, and everyone in between for being too permissive, for allowing the government whatever eavesdropping powers it requested. Indeed, its reputation for granting every eavesdropping request made by the government is so widespread that it has long been ridiculed as the "Rubber-Stamp Court."

Relevant statistics more than support those criticisms. According to figures compiled by the Federation of American Scientists, from 1978 until 2001—the year President Bush ordered eavesdropping outside of the law—the government submitted a total of 13,102 requests to the FISA court to eavesdrop on Americans. The FISA court *approved every single request* and only modified the requested warrant on a grand total of two occasions.

Nevertheless, the FISA court still performed an extremely important function: It ensured that presidents were not eavesdropping on Americans in secret, but rather with the knowledge of at least one federal judge on the

FISA court. And when a president knows that a FISA judge will be aware of any eavesdropping he orders, the opportunity for abuse is greatly diminished, if not eliminated. The severe abuses of the 1960s and 1970s essentially disappeared once FISA was enacted. Presidents were able to engage in legitimate eavesdropping as aggressively and potently as ever before, but their abuses were greatly diminished by oversight.

FISA worked exceptionally well under presidential administrations of each party. It worked all the way until October 2001, when President Bush quietly decided to order the NSA to eavesdrop on Americans in violation of FISA.

The significance of that decision is *not* that the president ordered eavesdropping to combat terrorism. The law not only allows that but encourages it by granting the government broad surveillance powers, and the NSA had already been eavesdropping under FISA prior to the time President Bush issued this order. Its significance was that the president ordered that surveillance be conducted *in violation of the law*—in total secrecy from the FISA courts. The choice which President Bush faced, then, was not eavesdropping versus not eavesdropping—it was between eavesdropping in compliance with the law versus eavesdropping illegally.

Beyond being plainly illegal, President Bush's decision is extremely difficult to understand from a policy and national security perspective. Whether the government eavesdrops in compliance with or in violation of FISA is irrelevant to whether it can engage in aggressive surveillance on Al Qaeda. FISA already allows full-scale eavesdropping on Al Qaeda. Violating FISA does not increase the government's ability to eavesdrop on terrorists at all. The only difference between obeying and violating FISA is that compliance with the law ensures that a court is aware of who is being eavesdropped on and how the eavesdropping is being conducted.

The president knew he was breaking the law, and he ordered eavesdropping without the knowledge of the FISA court anyway. That fact, by itself, makes his conduct inexcusable. As a report from the January 9, 2006, issue of *Time* magazine detailed:

> It didn't take long [after 9/11] before an aggressive idea emerged from the circle of administration hawks. Liberalize the rules for domestic spying, they urged. Free the National Security Agency (NSA) to use its powerful listening technology to eavesdrop on terrorist suspects

on U.S. soil without having to seek a warrant for every phone number it tracked. But because of a 1978 law that forbids the NSA to conduct no-warrant surveillance inside the U.S., the new policy would require one of two steps. The first was to revise the law. The other was to ignore it. In the end, George Bush tried the first. When that failed, he opted for the second.

The claim that at some point the Bush administration somehow tried to "revise" the law to eliminate the warrant requirement is unsubstantiated, as no members of Congress report having received any such requests from the White House. But if that claim is true—if the administration did attempt to induce Congress to allow warrantless eavesdropping on Americans but Congress refused—then the administration's lawbreaking is even more inexcusable, since Congress's refusal to amend the law amounted to a clear statement that it did not and would not authorize warrantless eavesdropping on Americans. Either way, the president's action was a criminal offense. Unconstrained by the mandates of the law, the president, as *Time* put it quite generously, opted to "ignore" the law.

Pattern of Deceit

During the four years since he issued the order, Bush and his top officials repeatedly assured the American people and the Congress—falsely—that the government was eavesdropping on Americans only in compliance with FISA. The record of this deceit should always begin with this statement by President Bush on April 20, 2004, as part of a speech he delivered in Buffalo, New York, while trying to convince Americans to reelect him to a second term. Addressing concerns about the government's increased eavesdropping powers, the president said:

> Secondly, there are such things as roving wiretaps. Now, by the way, *any time* you hear the United States government talking about wiretap, it requires—a wiretap requires a court order. Nothing has changed, by the way. When we're talking about chasing down terrorists, we're talking about getting a court order before we do so.

Coming from someone who had specifically authorized wiretaps without a court order, that statement cannot be seen as anything other than deliberate deceit. And he made this statement, or virtually identical statements, numerous other times throughout 2004 and 2005.

The president's statements are among the clearest, but by no means the only, examples of deceit from his administration on this issue. In July 2002, several senators—including Republicans Jon Kyl and Michael DeWine and Democrat Charles Schumer—had introduced amendments to FISA that would expand the government's eavesdropping powers. The senators scheduled hearings on their amendments before the Senate Intelligence Committee—which oversees even the most classified and secret government intelligence programs—and the Bush administration sent the Justice Department's James A. Baker to testify. Baker, under oath, assured the committee that the Senate could liberalize FISA without worrying about incursions into civil liberties because, he told them, the administration only eavesdrops with judicial approval:

> So you would be, you know, connecting electronic surveillance and potentially physical search of those targets and that raises all the same kinds of civil liberties questions that FISA does to begin with. But nevertheless, you would have had—before you get to that point, you would have had a finding by a neutral and detached magistrate, and indeed in this case a sitting federal judge, district court judge, that all of the requirements of the statute are met and that there's probable cause to believe that this individual is engaged in international terrorism activities, or activities in preparation therefor.

What Baker swore to the Senate committee (and, by implication, to all Americans)—that no eavesdropping occurs without a federal judge's approval—was completely false, whether Baker knew it or not.

Attorney General Alberto Gonzales peddled this same deceit as well. As *The Washington Post* reported on January 31, 2006, Gonzales was specifically asked by Senator Russ Feingold at his confirmation hearing in January 2005 whether the president had the power to engage in warrantless eavesdropping. Gonzales assured Feingold that the administration does not engage in activities forbidden by congressional law and the question was therefore "hypothetical." Here is the unambiguous exchange referenced by the *Post* article:

FEINGOLD: In the August 2002 memorandum, the Justice Department concludes that the president, as commander in chief, may authorize interrogations that violate the criminal laws prohibiting torture and that the Congress may not constitutionally outlaw such activity when it's authorized by the president. This is the claim, essentially, that the president is above the law so long as he is acting in the interests of national security. . . .

You also, I am told, said that many presidents have asserted the power not to enforce a statute that they believe is unconstitutional. But there is a difference between a president deciding not to enforce a statute which he thinks is unconstitutional and a president claiming to authorize individuals to break the law by torturing individuals or taking other illegal action.

So what I want to do is press you on that, because I think, perhaps, you've misunderstood the question. And it's an important one. It goes to a very basic principle of the country that no one, not even the president of the United States, is above the law. . . .

The question here is: What is your view regarding the president's constitutional authority to authorize violations of the criminal law, duly enacted statutes that may have been on the books for many years, when acting as commander in chief? Does he have such authority? The question you have been asked is not about a hypothetical statute in the future that the president might think is unconstitutional; it's about our laws and international treaty obligations concerning torture. The torture memo answered that question in the affirmative. And my colleagues and I would like your answer on that today.

And I also would like you to answer this: *Does the president, in your opinion, have the authority, acting as commander in chief, to authorize warrantless searches of Americans' homes and wiretaps of their conversations in violation of the criminal and foreign intelligence surveillance statutes of this country?*

GONZALES: Senator, the August 30th memo has been withdrawn. It has been rejected, including that section regarding the commander in chief authority to ignore the criminal statutes. So it's been rejected by the executive branch. I categorically reject it.

And in addition to that, as I've said repeatedly today, this administration does not engage in torture and will not condone torture. And so what we're really discussing is a hypothetical situation that . . .

FEINGOLD: Judge Gonzales, I've asked a broader question. I'm asking whether, in general, the president has constitutional authority—does he at least in theory have the authority to authorize violations of the criminal law when there are duly enacted statutes, simply because he's commander in chief? Does he have that power?

GONZALES: Senator, in my judgment, you phrase it as sort of a hypothetical situation. I would have to know what is the national interest that the president may have to consider.

What I'm saying is, it is impossible to me, based upon the question as you've presented it to me, to answer that question. [Emphasis added.]

As he gave these answers, Gonzales, who was the White House legal counsel in 2001, knew that President Bush had ordered the NSA to engage in surveillance without seeking FISA court approval. And yet, when Feingold asked him whether the president can "authorize warrantless searches of Americans' homes and wiretaps of their conversations in violation of the criminal and foreign intelligence surveillance statutes of this country," Gonzales, under oath, assured the Senate that this was purely a "hypothetical situation."

The administration repeatedly concealed its violations of the law, deliberately misleading Congress and the American public to believe that it was eavesdropping on Americans only with the approval of the FISA court. It allowed the Senate to go through the embarrassing spectacle of assuming that the administration was complying with FISA laws and that the Senate therefore had authority to regulate the administration's eavesdropping. It even encouraged that illusion by participating in the Senate hearings on proposed FISA amendments and pretending that what the Senate decided would actually have an impact on the administration's eavesdropping activities.

An institutional humiliation greater than this is difficult to imagine. Here, for instance, is what Senator Bob Graham, the then-chairman of the

Intelligence Committee, said when opening the hearings on these proposed FISA amendments in 2002:

> The two bills that we are here to discuss today will provide additional changes to FISA for the purpose of reducing both the nature and scope of the showing the government must make to obtain a surveillance order against suspected terrorists inside the United States who are neither citizens nor legal resident aliens. As we did with the changes made in FISA last year, the Congress must examine revisions of this nature to assure that they strike the proper balance between enhancing our ability to fight terrorism while protecting our privacy and liberties. That is the purpose of the hearing today.

Similarly, here is what Senator Schumer said in explaining why he thought his FISA amendments were so important:

> Now, Senator Kyl's and my goal, quite simply, is to make it easier for law enforcement to get warrants against non-U.S. citizens who are preparing to commit acts of terrorism. . . .
>
> I believe the Vice President, the FBI Director, and the Secretary of Defense when they say other attacks are planned. Right now there may well be terrorists plotting on American soil. We may have all kinds of reasons to believe that specific individuals in our communities are preparing to commit acts of terrorism, but we can't do the surveillance we need to do because we can't tie them to a foreign power. . . .
>
> It's important to note that if our bill becomes law it will immeasurably aid law enforcement without exposing American citizens and permanent legal resident aliens to the slightest additional surveillance. This law will only affect non-citizens and non-green card holders. And the language we're proposing is the same language the administration sent up here during the debate over the Intelligence Authorization Bill. Attorney General Ashcroft has given his stamp of approval.

Ashcroft, then, expressly told Senator Schumer that he supported the FISA amendments knowing full well that the administration did not need them; after all, the administration had already decided that it had the power to engage in whatever eavesdropping it wanted, whether the laws passed by Congress approved of it or, as was the case with FISA, criminalized it. Various administration officials, from the Justice Department, the FBI, and the CIA, testified at these hearings as though it mattered what Congress did with regard to amending FISA. They all gave the impression that it was Congress, through FISA, that determined the scope of the administration's eavesdropping powers, and never once stated, suggested, implied, or even hinted that the administration, months before, had decided that it could eavesdrop far beyond the confines of that law.

The administration's claim that it "briefed" congressional leaders on the details of the secret NSA program has been vigorously disputed by some of them, including former senator Bob Graham, who, as these 2002 hearings make clear, was operating under the assumption that the administration was eavesdropping only in compliance with the law. Moreover, even in the administration's rendition of these "briefings," those members of Congress were given few details about the program, were unaware of who was being eavesdropped on, and were repeatedly warned that any discussion of what they were told would be a criminal offense, because the information was classified.

Nevertheless, several members of Congress did object privately to the program, one reason being that they weren't given enough information to assess its propriety or legality. Those objections were simply ignored by the administration. What is beyond dispute is that nobody outside of the executive branch knew how these powers were being used and that the president repeatedly misled Congress to believe that he was following the law.

All of this deceit, independent of the lawbreaking issues, is scandalous in itself. Lying under oath to Congress—as Gonzales plainly did when answering Feingold and as Baker likely did when he testified that the administration only eavesdrops with warrants—is itself a criminal offense. Moreover, it is the greatest breach of trust for a president to assuage public fears about eavesdropping by knowingly making false statements about the government's conduct.

Unilateral Actions

The heart of the matter is that the president broke the law, deliberately and repeatedly, no matter what his rationale was for doing so. We do not have a system of government in which the president has the right to violate laws, even if he believes doing so will produce good results. Nonetheless, with regard to the NSA scandal, one question still remains: *Why* did President Bush choose to break the law?

On February 24, 2006, Democratic members of the House Judiciary Committee submitted a series of written questions to the Bush administration, seeking to learn the nature and scope of the secret eavesdropping program. Among the questions were these: How many persons in the United States have been targets of the warrantless surveillance program? How does the NSA staff determine whether such targets are working in support of Al Qaeda? How much time and money has been spent searching or seizing the phone calls or e-mails of people in the United States, and how much of this has been spent on people who have never been charged with any crime? Were the Justice Department and solicitor general's office aware of this program, and if so, when did they become aware? Did any of the lawyers inside the Justice Department object to these eavesdropping activities on the ground that they were illegal?

The Bush administration sent back a response on March 26, 2006. While it refused to provide any information as to the most basic questions, it did provide a quite revealing (though largely unnoticed) answer to one question: "What is the rationale for authorizing a program to conduct surveillance in a matter that does not require prior judicial review by the FISA Court?" In response, the Justice Department acknowledged:

> Among the advantages offered by the [president's warrantless eavesdropping program] compared to FISA is *who* makes the probable cause determination and how many layers of review must occur *before* surveillance begins." [Emphasis in original.]

This candid admission provides critical insight into what truly motivated the president to eavesdrop on Americans outside of FISA. What possible reason is there for refusing to obtain court approval when the court never denies that approval or impedes eavesdropping efforts in any way?

As Congress devised the law, the FISA court plays two critical, independent functions—not just warrant approval but also, more critically, judicial oversight. FISA's truly meaningful check on abuse in the eavesdropping process is that the president is prevented from engaging in improper eavesdropping *because he knows that every instance of eavesdropping he orders will be known to a federal judge*—a high-level judicial officer who is not subject to the president's authority and whose constitutional duties are separate from the president's.

It is precisely that safeguard which President Bush simply abolished by fiat. In effect, President Bush changed the law all by himself, replacing the federal judges with his own employees at the NSA and abolishing the approval and warrant process entirely.

To describe that conduct is to illustrate its jaw-dropping lawlessness and corruption. It ought to go without saying that, at least in America, the president does not have the right to unilaterally change laws that he does not like. He cannot simply abolish his least favorite provisions and replace them with ones he likes better.

That we have a profound and serious crisis in our country as a result of this presidential lawlessness should not be a controversial proposition subject to political posturing by either party. If the president claims the right—as he manifestly has—to violate laws that he does not want to be constrained by, and to thereby freely engage in behavior which has been expressly criminalized for decades in this country, then, by definition, we are a country in which the president has seized powers that could not be any more alien, or threatening, to the defining principles and constitutional values on which our system of government has been based since its founding.

CHAPTER TWO

The Power of One

The National Security Agency eavesdropping scandal is not an isolated act of lawbreaking. It is an outgrowth of an ideology of lawlessness that has been adopted by the Bush administration as its governing doctrine. Others include the incarceration in military prisons of U.S. citizens who were not charged with any crime or even allowed access to a lawyer, the use of legally prohibited torture techniques, and the establishment of a military detention center in Guantanamo Bay, a no-man's-land that the administration claims is beyond the reach of U.S. law. In the media and the public mind, these issues have been seen in isolation, as though they are unconnected.

In fact, all of these controversial actions can be traced to a single cause, a shared root. They are grounded in, and are the by-product of, an unprecedented and truly radical theory of presidential power that, at its core, maintains that the president's power is literally unlimited and absolute in matters relating to terrorism or national security.

Using the 2001 terrorist attacks as the justification, the Bush administration has expressly embraced theories, generated by ideologues in its Justice Department, that are simply alien to the American system of government. The administration has claimed—and has repeatedly asserted and applied the principle—that any presidential actions relating to terrorism or security cannot be limited by Congress, the courts, or the American people. Decisions about such matters are, to quote the principal Bush administration document that legitimized these theories, "for the President alone to make."

The notion that one of the three branches of government—executive, judicial, and legislative—can exercise power unchecked by the other two is precisely what America's founders sought, first and foremost, to preclude. And the fear that a president would seize power unchecked by the law or by the other branches—in the manner of the British king—was the driving force behind the clear and numerous constitutional limitations placed on presidential power. The Bush administration simply does not recognize these limitations. This raises the question of why the White House believes it can ignore the laws of the land, and where that belief comes from.

The King and Yoo

The president's secret order to have the NSA eavesdrop on American citizens without warrants, in violation of FISA, was first reported by *The New York Times* on December 15, 2005. Two days later, the *Times* published an article describing the rationale behind the president's belief, specifically identifying "a Sept. 25, 2001 memorandum" by John Yoo:

> A single, fiercely debated legal principle lies behind nearly every major initiative in the Bush administration's war on terror, scholars say: the sweeping assertion of the powers of the presidency.
>
> From the government's detention of Americans as "enemy combatants" to the just-disclosed eavesdropping in the United States without court warrants, the administration has relied on an unusually expansive interpretation of the president's authority.

Although most Americans have likely never heard of the "Yoo memorandum," no single document has more greatly influenced how our executive branch has been functioning for the last five years. The theories of presidential power in that memo have been officially adopted by the Bush administration, and they could not be more hostile to the traditions and core political values of the United States.

Long before the 9/11 attacks, certain far-right legal theorists had argued that the president has virtually unchecked and absolute powers in all matters pertaining to the defense of the nation—including the power to violate the law if he deems it in the national interest to do so. Many of these men had been advocating these theories since as far back as the Nixon administration, but—in the wake of Watergate and the governmental abuses detailed by the Church Committee—their theories were viewed as radical and extremist, and they had currency only on the farthest fringes of legal scholarship and political ideology.

But on the day of the 9/11 attacks, it so happened that one zealous believer in those theories, John Yoo, occupied the position of deputy assistant attorney general in the Justice Department's Office of Legal Counsel (OLC). The OLC may be the most powerful office in Washington that most people have never heard of. It produces legal memoranda that, upon their issuance, become the official position of the Justice Department and the entire executive branch.

And John Yoo was the ideal person to provide the justification the White House wanted in order to drastically expand the powers of the president and eliminate longstanding restrictions on how those powers could be exercised. As a December 26, 2005, *Washington Post* profile of him put it, Yoo became "a principal interpreter of laws and the Constitution for the Bush team." The profile also said this about Yoo:

> Known for his belief in a strong presidency, he joined the Justice Department's Office of Legal Counsel, which advises the attorney general and the White House, in July 2001. Two months later came the terrorist attacks and the rush to respond. Soon, Yoo found his audience in the highest echelons of the White House, where the president and vice president already tended to see the courts, Congress and international conventions as constraints on the conduct of foreign affairs and national security.
>
> "He was the right person in the right place at the right time," said Georgetown University's David Cole, a constitutional scholar and administration critic. "Here was someone who had made his career developing arguments for unchecked power, who could cut-and-paste from his law review articles into memos that essentially told the president, 'You can do what you want.'"

On September 25, 2001, Yoo authored the now-famous memo in response to the president's request for an "opinion as to the scope of the President's authority to take military action in response to the terrorist attacks on the United States on September 11, 2001," as the memo itself stated. The bulk of the memo was devoted to an analysis of the president's power to direct the movement of the armed forces as part of foreign wars. But Yoo contended that the president's powers were not confined only to battlefields or wars; he emphatically argued that the president has the power to make *any decisions* with regard to all matters relating to defense of the country and that neither the Congress, nor the courts, nor any longstanding laws can restrict or limit those decisions in any way.

Yoo pushed the theory into wholly uncharted waters by arguing that these unlimited presidential powers can be used against U.S. citizens on U.S. soil. That theory, which became the official view of the Bush administration, was most concisely—and chillingly—conveyed by the last three sentences of Yoo's memo:

> In both the War Powers Resolution and the Joint Resolution, Congress has recognized the President's authority to use force in circumstances such as those created by the September 11 incidents. Neither statute, however, can place any limits on the President's determinations as to any terrorist threat, the amount of military force to be used in response, or the method, timing, and nature of the response. These decisions, under our Constitution, are for the President alone to make.

Put simply, this constitutes a radical departure from everything that has defined the United States since its founding. The notion that decisions about what actions our country takes "are for the President alone to make"—without interference from Congress, the courts, or the American people—is wholly antithetical to the system of government under which Americans have lived for more than two centuries. Under such a theory, if Congress enacts a law making it a criminal offense to eavesdrop on Americans without judicial oversight and approval, then the president is free to violate that law. If the American people decide that they want to criminalize the use of torture and Congress enacts legislation banning torture, the president can disregard the law and use torture anyway.

In one sense, this theory of limitless presidential power is not new. It has its origins in the worldview of former president Richard M. Nixon, who notoriously endorsed the idea in a May 1977 interview with journalist David Frost, three years after being forced from office:

> FROST: So what in a sense you're saying is that there are certain situations . . . where the president can decide that it's in the best interests of the nation or something, and do something illegal.

NIXON: Well, when the president does it that means that it is not illegal.

FROST: By definition.

NIXON: Exactly. If the president, for example, approves something because of the national security, or in this case because of a threat to internal peace and order of significant magnitude, then the president's decision in that instance is one that enables those who carry it out, to carry it out without violating a law. Otherwise they're in an impossible position.

But not even the Nixon administration asserted this lawbreaking power as overtly, as unabashedly, and as consistently as the Bush administration. Rather than applying this theory of unchecked executive power to a single case, the Bush administration has arrogated unto itself this monarchical power as a general proposition, applicable to each and every issue that can be said to relate, however generally, to the undeclared "war on terror."

The first time this theory was invoked—at least as far as we now know—was when President Bush, in October 2001, ordered the NSA to eavesdrop on American citizens in violation of FISA. But this was by no means the only time. Over the next four years, the Bush administration repeatedly asserted that it had the right to seize powers that cannot be limited or restricted in any way by the courts, by Congress, or by the law. In short, President Bush has claimed the defining powers of a king.

Matter of Decree

The president-as-monarch theory made its next appearance when the Bush administration decided that it could incarcerate American citizens in military prisons without any charges being brought against them and without even allowing them access to lawyers.

Yaser Esam Hamdi is an American citizen, born in Louisiana in 1980. He was found and detained by the U.S. military in Afghanistan in November 2001. The military claimed that he was working with the Taliban, while Hamdi claimed that he was there to perform relief work. The Bush administration placed him in the military detention center it constructed in Guantanamo Bay in Cuba. Upon learning that Hamdi is a U.S. citizen, the administration, in early 2002, transferred him to a naval brig in South Carolina.

In secret, President Bush signed a decree accusing Hamdi of being an "enemy combatant," and ordered his administration to keep Hamdi imprisoned in a military prison. Hamdi was not charged with any crime and was not allowed access to a lawyer. He was simply locked away and allowed no contact with anyone, and the administration asserted the right to detain Hamdi under these circumstances *indefinitely.*

This is worth repeating: An American citizen was locked in prison, not allowed any contact with family, friends, or a lawyer, not charged with any specific crime, and not allowed to come before any judge, all based on a secret decree by President Bush that he was an "enemy combatant." Worse, the administration claimed that the president's decree could not be reviewed by any court. They insisted that Hamdi had no right to challenge the decree or even to see the charges against him, and that they could keep him imprisoned for as long as they wanted without giving him any opportunity in court to have the allegations reviewed or to defend himself from the charges.

The administration thus brought to life one of the most un-American nightmares imaginable. In many countries, citizens can be taken by police and thrown in jail without charges on the orders of a dictator. But in the United States, a citizen cannot be imprisoned without being charged with a crime and given access to a lawyer, and then being convicted of crimes by a jury of one's peers. The president does not have—and never has had—the power to single-handedly order American citizens imprisoned with no charges and no ability to make their case. President Bush simply claimed this right based on the administration's theories that the president's power in these areas is unlimited, absolute, and unreviewable by an American court.

For two years, Hamdi was kept in solitary confinement, without a lawyer or any other access to the outside world. He was finally allowed a lawyer only after his father brought suit in a federal court requesting a ruling that as an American citizen, Hamdi had the constitutional right not to be imprisoned without being charged and convicted of a crime by a jury of his peers. Hamdi's father pointed out in the lawsuit that the mere fact that the president *claimed* that Hamdi committed crimes is not enough—nor has it ever been enough—in the American system of justice to imprison an American citizen. Hamdi's family denied the president's accusation that Hamdi was working with the Taliban, insisting that he had traveled to Afghanistan to engage in relief work.

The Bush administration argued that neither the courts nor Congress has the power to review or limit the president's decisions in any matters concerning terrorism or national security. *Hamdi v. Rumsfeld* eventually made its way to the U.S. Supreme Court, where in 2004 the court summarized the administration's position as follows:

> The Government contends that Hamdi is an "enemy combatant," and that this status justifies holding him in the United States indefinitely—without formal charges or proceedings—unless and until it makes the determination that access to counsel or further process is warranted.

As the court recounted, the Bush administration not only argued that the courts have no power even to review any decision made by the president to imprison U.S. citizens with no charges, but also claimed that:

> "Respect for separation of powers and the limited institutional capabilities of courts in matters of military decision-making in connection with an ongoing conflict" ought to eliminate entirely any individual process, restricting the courts to investigating only whether legal authorization exists for the broader detention scheme.

Put another way, the administration argued that once the president, *in secret*, deems a U.S. citizen to be an enemy combatant, that designation cannot be challenged by the imprisoned citizen.

Not only are the courts without any power to review the president's decrees to imprison U.S. citizens, the Bush administration insisted that Congress as well lacks the power to limit or regulate these imprisonments in any way, because the president possesses this power "inherently" under the Constitution. As the Supreme Court put it in *Hamdi:*

The Government maintains that no explicit congressional authorization is required, because the Executive possesses plenary authority to detain pursuant to Article II of the Constitution.

The Supreme Court also pointed out the consequences for Hamdi if the court were to accept the Bush administration's position that the president had the right to hold him until the "war" was over:

> As the Government concedes, "given its unconventional nature, the current conflict is unlikely to end with a formal cease-fire agreement." *Ibid.* The prospect Hamdi raises is therefore not far-fetched. If the Government does not consider this unconventional war won for two generations, and if it maintains during that time that Hamdi might, if released, rejoin forces fighting against the United States, then the position it has taken throughout the litigation of this case suggests that Hamdi's detention could last for the rest of his life.

The Bush administration, then, claimed the right to consign American citizens to *life in prison* without charges, without access to a lawyer, without any opportunity for the citizen even to make his case.

The U.S. Supreme Court recognized the administration's conduct as a profound assault on basic constitutional liberties. The Court ruled, on April 28, 2004, that while Congress had granted the administration the authority to detain citizens as enemy combatants, the U.S. Constitution barred the president from imprisoning them without affording them the opportunity to contest the accusations in court. The Court explained:

> [I]t would turn our system of checks and balances on its head to suggest that a citizen could not make his way to court with a challenge to the factual basis for his detention by his government, simply because the Executive opposes making available such a challenge.

The majority opinion, authored by Justice Sandra Day O'Connor, held that while the president was given the power to detain "enemy combatants" when Congress authorized him to use military force in Afghanistan, the administration could not deny them the right to contest the validity of the president's decree. Only one of the nine justices, Clarence Thomas, disagreed with that conclusion.

Justice Antonin Scalia, who usually sides with the Bush administration and is a longtime advocate of broad presidential powers, objected that the court's decision did not go far enough in finding the president's conduct towards Hamdi unconstitutional. Justice Scalia wrote a long and impassioned opinion making clear that the United States was founded upon a rebellion against exactly the powers asserted by President Bush—the power to imprison citizens with no charges based solely on the decree of the ruler—and that there is no more basic American value than the prohibition on citizens being imprisoned by their government based on a secret, monarchlike decree.

Scalia explained that other than in times of national emergency, when the U.S. Constitution allows Congress to suspend the right to challenge one's imprisonment (something that has not occurred since the Nineteenth Century), no elected official has the right to unilaterally and secretly order the imprisonment of American citizens without charging them with a crime. Scalia added that no U.S. citizen can ever be held as an "enemy combatant," because a citizen who is truly fighting a war against America can be charged with treason and given all due process to defend himself. As Scalia put it: "The very core of liberty secured by our Anglo-Saxon system of separated powers has been freedom from indefinite imprisonment at the will of the Executive."

Revealingly, once the Bush administration was required by the Supreme Court to actually prove in court that Hamdi was in fact an enemy combatant, it refused to do so. Instead—after keeping Hamdi incarcerated in solitary confinement for two years and claiming that he was so dangerous that no charges even needed to be brought—the Bush administration simply released Hamdi from its custody and allowed him to return to Saudi Arabia, where he had spent much of his childhood. Hamdi was required as part of the release agreement to renounce his U.S. citizenship, a rather ironic action given that Hamdi had, over the prior two years, been denied his basic citizenship rights.

And so, after repeatedly insisting that Hamdi was so dangerous that he should be imprisoned indefinitely—possibly for life—the president decided to simply release Hamdi rather than prove his guilt in a court of law.

The Case of the "Dirty Bomber"

On May 8, 2002, Jose Padilla, an American citizen born in New York City who then moved to Chicago's West Side, was arrested by U.S. marshals at O'Hare International Airport in Chicago. The same day, Attorney General John Ashcroft hastily called a news conference in Russia, where he was visiting, and accused Padilla of involvement in a plot to smuggle a radiological weapon into the U.S. and detonate it in one of America's cities. Ashcroft claimed that the Bush administration had prevented a radiological attack by arresting Padilla.

As a result of Ashcroft's press conference, which was broadcast around the world, Padilla was instantaneously crowned "The Dirty Bomber." His guilt was a foregone conclusion, based exclusively on the government's accusations. Administration officials also leaked to the media that Padilla had been plotting to blow up apartment buildings in the United States with natural gas pipelines.

On June 9, 2002, President Bush signed yet another secret order, this one decreeing Padilla to be an enemy combatant, and as a result, he was transferred to a military prison in South Carolina and subjected to the same "black hole" treatment that Hamdi received—placed in solitary confinement, not formally charged with any crime, denied access to a lawyer. Jose Padilla remained in military prison for the next three and a half years without being charged with any crime.

Very early in the case, it was clear that the evidence that Padilla was involved in a plot to detonate radiological bombs was extremely sketchy and unreliable. *Newsweek* reported on August 19, 2002:

> Much of the evidence, officials say, comes from a single, less-than-reliable informant: Abu Zubaydah, a former chief of Qaeda training camps who was picked up in Pakistan last fall. Zubaydah told interrogators about a U.S.-born Qaeda recruit who, along with two accomplices, had talked to him in Afghanistan last year about a plan to build a radiological dispersion device or "dirty bomb" that could create mass terror inside the United States. Apparent confirmation came when U.S. forces found photos of Padilla in a Qaeda safe house and computers showing that someone—believed to be Padilla—had

been cruising the Internet checking out Web sites of U.S. university labs and hospitals where radiological material could be acquired.

But none of it was enough for the Justice Department to bring charges against Padilla. Officials now acknowledge that the plot had never moved much beyond talk. If Padilla had any accomplices in the United States, FBI officials say, they have never been found or even identified. The idea of a plot was "blown out of proportion," said one U.S. intelligence official.

But whether there was any evidence that these charges were actually true was irrelevant to the Bush administration. They decided that they did not need to charge him with anything or prove to any judge that he was guilty of any crime. President Bush had decreed that Padilla was an enemy combatant, and that was enough to incarcerate him in a military prison without charges.

In one sense, the Bush administration's assertion of power to imprison Padilla was more extreme than its move to imprison Hamdi. Unlike Hamdi, who was detained in Afghanistan and then brought to a military brig in the United States, Padilla was arrested on U.S. soil. And to justify such imprisonment, the Bush administration expressly asserted the same theory of absolute presidential power—that as long as some connection can be shown to terrorism or national security, the president has the power to do *anything,* even to U.S. citizens on U.S. soil, and neither the courts nor the Congress can interfere, overrule, or even review his actions. One of the two appellate courts that ultimately did review Padilla's incarceration, the Second Circuit Court of Appeals in Manhattan, summarized the Bush administration's positions as follows: "The administration claims that 'indefinite detention was a proper exercise of the President's power as Commander-in-Chief'; that President Bush's power 'encompasses the detention of United States citizens seized on U.S. soil'; and that this power may even be 'exercised without a formal declaration of war by Congress.'"

Just as it did in Hamdi's case, the U. S. Supreme Court announced in 2005 that it would rule on the constitutionality of the Bush administration's imprisonment of Padilla. The deadline for the administration to make its written argument to the Court was November 28, 2005. The administration failed to comply with this deadline. Instead, on November

22, 2005—just over a week before the brief was due, and three and a half years after Padilla was first placed in solitary confinement—the administration filed a criminal indictment against him in federal court. Astonishingly, after announcing to the world that Padilla was a "dirty bomber" who tried to smuggle a radiological bomb into the United States, the Bush administration indicted him on vague and unspecified charges of conspiracy to commit terrorist acts. None of those charges had anything to do with the accusation that he had been involved in a plot to smuggle a dirty bomb into the country. Once again, when the Bush administration was forced to prove its accusations in a court of law, it simply walked away from them.

As *The New York Times* reported on November 23, 2005:

> The indictment [filed against Mr. Padilla] is narrower in scope than the previous accusations that the Bush administration has made publicly against Mr. Padilla, and it makes no direct mention of Al Qaeda or the more far-ranging plots on American soil that the administration had linked to him.
>
> After Mr. Padilla was arrested in May 2002 at O'Hare Airport in Chicago, John Ashcroft, then the attorney general, interrupted a trip to Moscow to announce on television that the authorities had foiled an effort by Mr. Padilla and other Qaeda operatives to detonate a radioactive or "dirty" bomb on American streets.
>
> In June 2004, senior Justice Department officials went further, using newly declassified documents—and statements they said Mr. Padilla had made in the military brig to his interrogators—to assert that he had plotted to blow up apartment buildings and hotels, perhaps in New York.
>
> But Attorney General Alberto R. Gonzales, announcing the criminal charges at a news conference on Tuesday, said Mr. Padilla's status as an enemy combatant and the previous accusations made against him by the administration were "legally irrelevant to the charges we're bringing today."

To understand the Bush administration's motive in bringing any charges at all against Padilla after three and a half years, we have to look at what the Justice Department did next. It immediately filed a brief with the

Supreme Court arguing that, because Padilla was no longer being held without charges in a military prison, the Court no longer needed to rule on the question of whether the Bush administration acted in violation of the U.S. Constitution in imprisoning him without due process. As the same *Times* article reported:

> The decision to remove Mr. Padilla from military custody and charge him in the civilian system averts what had threatened to be a constitutional showdown over the president's authority to detain him and other American citizens as enemy combatants without formal charges.
>
> The administration had faced a deadline next Monday to file its legal arguments with the Supreme Court in the Padilla case, which the Justice Department said it now considers "moot."

As a result of the Bush administration's sudden filing of criminal charges, Court of Appeals Judge J. Michael Luttig—a right-wing federal judge who had ruled in favor of the administration on numerous occasions, including in the Padilla case—issued a scathing ruling on December 21, 2005, condemning the actions of the administration in the Padilla case, saying they "create at least an appearance that the government may be attempting to avoid consideration of our decision by the Supreme Court." Judge Luttig also expressed great skepticism about both the administration's motives and legal theories:

> [A]s the government surely must understand, although the various facts it has asserted are not necessarily inconsistent or without basis, its actions have left not only the impression that Padilla may have been held for these years, even if justifiably, by mistake—an impression we would have thought the government could ill afford to leave extant.
>
> They have left the impression that the government may even have come to the belief that the principle in reliance upon which it has detained Padilla for this time, that the President possesses the authority to detain enemy combatants who enter into this country for the purpose of attacking America and its citizens from within, can, in the end, yield to expediency with little or no cost to its con-

duct of the war against terror—an impression we would have thought the government likewise could ill afford to leave extant.

And these impressions have been left, we fear, at what may ultimately prove to be substantial cost to the government's credibility before the courts, to whom it will one day need to argue again in support of a principle of assertedly like importance and necessity to the one that it seems to abandon today. While there could be an objective that could command such a price as all of this, it is difficult to imagine what that objective would be.

Despite the administration's argument that Padilla's claims were now moot, his lawyers still urged the Supreme Court to rule on whether the administration's imprisonment of Padilla was legal. After all, as the *Times* article put it, the Padilla case presented a "constitutional showdown over the president's authority to detain him and other American citizens as enemy combatants without formal charges."

On April 3, 2006, the U.S. Supreme Court—with two new Bush appointees, John Roberts and Samuel Alito, in the majority —decided by a 6-3 vote that, in light of the charges finally brought against Padilla, the Court should not rule on the legality of the Bush administration's actions unless they attempted again to imprison him without charges—for instance, by rescinding the charges filed against him and then retransferring him into military custody. Justice Ruth Bader Ginsburg, one of the three dissenting justices, explained that the issues raised by the case "were of profound importance to the nation," and said that "although the government has recently lodged charges against Padilla in a civilian court, nothing prevents the executive from returning to the road it earlier constructed and defended." Justice John Paul Stevens had previously said that what is "at stake in this case is nothing less than the essence of a free society."

And so the Bush administration has preserved for itself, at least for now, the ability to continue to arrest and imprison U.S. citizens on U.S. soil and hold them indefinitely as "enemy combatants."

There is a clear commonality between the administration's actions in the Hamdi and Padilla cases. Once it was forced to defend in a court of law the accusations the president had insisted were unreviewable, the administration chose to simply drop them.

When the Bush administration backed off from charging Padilla with being a dirty bomber, the question remained: Why did they hold him for three and a half years, saying he was about to detonate a radioactive bomb and blow up buildings using natural gas pipelines, and then not charge him with those crimes? The answer to that question revealed yet another low point for the Bush administration and yet another assault on American values and principles.

Confessions by Waterboarding

A December 24, 2005, article in *The New York Times* reported new and truly remarkable facts about the Padilla case. The Bush administration, said the article, had obtained the information on which the accusations against Padilla were based *by torturing the two sources who provided it.* As the *Times* reported:

> The Bush administration decided to charge Jose Padilla with less serious crimes because it was unwilling to allow testimony from two senior members of Al Qaeda who had been subjected to harsh questioning, current and former government officials said Wednesday.
>
> The two senior members were the main sources linking Mr. Padilla to a plot to bomb targets in the United States, the officials said. . . .
>
> One review, completed in spring 2004 by the C.I.A. inspector general, found that Mr. Mohammed [one of the two members] had been subjected to excessive use of a technique involving near drowning in the first months after his capture, American intelligence officials said.
>
> Another review, completed in April 2003 by American intelligence agencies shortly after Mr. Mohammed's capture, assessed the quality of his information from initial questioning as "Precious Truths, Surrounded by a Bodyguard of Lies." . . . .
>
> The fact that the C.I.A. inspector general's report criticized as excessive the use of interrogation techniques on Mr. Mohammed had not previously been disclosed.

The use of torture as an interrogation tool by the United States is yet another by-product of the president's belief, grounded in the infamous Yoo memorandum, that nothing can limit the president's decisions with regard to terrorism. The president is free to use torture, opined Yoo, regardless of whether it is illegal under the laws of the United States.

Shortly after the 9/11 attacks, Yoo had begun arguing that the Geneva Conventions—which, as a ratified treaty, constitute binding American law with regard to treatment of prisoners captured in war—did not have to be complied with by the president when it came to Taliban soldiers or Al Qaeda members. He then took a further step in purportedly freeing the president from legal prohibitions on the use of torture by producing another memo, which created a new definition of "torture," allowing a whole slew of methods which had long been banned in the United States. As Jane Mayer reported in her February 14, 2005, *New Yorker* article:

> Further, an August, 2002, memo written largely by Yoo but signed by Assistant Attorney General Jay S. Bybee argued that torture required the intent to inflict suffering "equivalent in intensity to the pain accompanying serious physical injury, such as organ failure, impairment of bodily function, or even death." According to the *Times*, a secret memo issued by administration lawyers authorized the C.I.A. to use novel interrogation methods—including "waterboarding," in which a suspect is bound and immersed in water until he nearly drowns. Dr. Allen Keller, the director of the Bellevue/ N.Y.U. Program for Survivors of Torture, told me that he had treated a number of people who had been subjected to such forms of near-asphyxiation, and he argued that it was indeed torture. Some victims were still traumatized years later, he said. One patient couldn't take showers, and panicked when it rained. "The fear of being killed is a terrifying experience," he said.

Consistent with his general view that there can be no limits on the president's conduct, Yoo made clear to Mayer that the president's unlimited power means that he is free to torture people, even if the law prohibits it. As Mayer recounted:

Yoo also argued that the Constitution granted the President plenary powers to override the U.N. Convention Against Torture when he is acting in the nation's defense—a position that has drawn dissent from many scholars. As Yoo saw it, Congress doesn't have the power to "tie the President's hands in regard to torture as an interrogation technique." He continued, "It's the core of the Commander-in-Chief function. They can't prevent the President from ordering torture."

When the United States signs a treaty that is ratified by the Senate, its mandates formally become part of federal law, binding on all Americans. In addition, by signing a treaty, the United States gives its word to the rest of the world that it will adhere to the commitments it is making. But none of that mattered to John Yoo or to the administration. After all, Yoo had already concluded, and the administration had already asserted, that the president was not bound to obey U.S. laws, notwithstanding his constitutional duty to see that they be "faithfully executed." Why should international treaties be any different?

Yoo's theories about the legal prohibitions on torture came to life and played a critical role in the lawless imprisonment of Padilla. According to a classified report obtained by ABC News, waterboarding was among the "interrogation techniques" used by the Bush administration against Al Qaeda member Khalid Sheik Mohammed when questioning him about Padilla. A November 18, 2005, report from ABC News described this technique, based upon a confidential CIA source:

> The prisoner is bound to an inclined board, feet raised and head slightly below the feet. Cellophane is wrapped over the prisoner's face and water is poured over him. Unavoidably, the gag reflex kicks in and a terrifying fear of drowning leads to almost instant pleas to bring the treatment to a halt.
>
> According to the sources, CIA officers who subjected themselves to the water boarding technique lasted an average of 14 seconds before caving in. They said al Qaeda's toughest prisoner, Khalid Sheik Mohammed, won the admiration of interrogators when he was able to last between two and two-and-a-half minutes before begging to confess.

"The person believes they are being killed, and as such, it really amounts to a mock execution, which is illegal under international law," said John Sifton of Human Rights Watch.

Setting aside moral issues regarding torture, intelligence officers recognize that the waterboarding technique produces information that is completely unreliable. The same ABC News report explained why:

The techniques are controversial among experienced intelligence agency and military interrogators. Many feel that a confession obtained this way is an unreliable tool. Two experienced officers have told ABC that there is little to be gained by these techniques that could not be more effectively gained by a methodical, careful, psychologically based interrogation.

According to a classified report prepared by the CIA Inspector General John Helgerwon and issued in 2004, the techniques "appeared to constitute cruel and degrading treatment under the [Geneva] convention," the New York Times reported on Nov. 9, 2005.

It is "bad interrogation. I mean you can get anyone to confess to anything if the torture's bad enough," said former CIA officer Bob Baer.

Larry Johnson, a former CIA officer and a deputy director of the State Department's office of counterterrorism, recently wrote in the *Los Angeles Times*, "What real CIA field officers know firsthand is that it is better to build a relationship of trust . . . than to extract quick confessions through tactics such as those used by the Nazis and the Soviets."

So, while the administration kept an American citizen locked away in solitary confinement for more than three years while it told the world that he was a dirty bomber, it knew, but concealed, that the accusations were based on statements gained through illegal methods of torture.

The Padilla case was by no means the only instance where the Bush administration employed illegal forms of torture to obtain highly suspect information. They used confessions extracted through similar methods as the basis for persuading the American people of the necessity of going to war in Iraq. The same ABC News report detailed:

According to CIA sources, Ibn al Shaykh al Libbi, after two weeks of enhanced interrogation, made statements that were designed to tell the interrogators what they wanted to hear. Sources say al Libbi had been subjected to each of the progressively harsher techniques in turn and finally broke after being waterboarded and then left to stand naked in his cold cell overnight, where he was doused with cold water at regular intervals.

His statements became part of the basis for the Bush administration claims that Iraq trained al Qaeda members to use biochemical weapons. Sources tell ABC that it was later established that al Libbi had no knowledge of such training or weapons and fabricated the statements because he was terrified of further harsh treatment.

"This is the problem with using the waterboard. They get so desperate that they begin telling you what they think you want to hear," one source said.

To recap: The Bush administration's oft-repeated mantra that Saddam Hussein was training Al Qaeda in the use of chemical weapons was based on "information" obtained through torture, which itself violates U.S. and international law. Nevertheless, the administration then took these "confessions" and used them to persuade Americans that the war in Iraq was necessary because Iraq was training Al Qaeda in the use of chemical weapons.

Tortured Legislation

In response to public outrage over the fact that the United States under the Bush administration has become a nation that tortures people, Republican Senator John McCain of Arizona introduced legislation in the fall of 2005 to ban the use of torture in every circumstance. The Bush administration vehemently argued against this legislation; Vice President Dick Cheney lobbied Congress to oppose it; and the president, who has not vetoed a single piece of legislation in the five years he has been president, even threatened to veto the legislation if the Republican-controlled Congress passed it.

Nevertheless, the Senate, on October 7, 2005, voted 90 to 9 to approve the ban on torture. And on December 15, 2005, the House approved the torture ban by a vote of 308 to 122. Because the lopsided nature of both votes made clear that any veto by the president would be overridden, the president was forced to abandon his threat. As a result, on December 30, 2005, the president signed the McCain bill into law, even though he opposed it.

Traditionally, when Congress passes a bill that the president then signs into law, it is incontrovertibly the law of the land, binding on everyone. But that was before the Bush administration conjured up its radical theories of unlimited presidential power. Now, even laws that are passed overwhelmingly by Congress *and signed into law by the president*—such as the ban on torture—cannot, in the view of the Bush administration, be binding on the president in any way.

On the day that President Bush signed the McCain torture ban, he issued a "signing statement"—a document sometimes issued by the president setting forth how he interprets the law and how he intends to execute it. Here is what President Bush said in his signing statement about whether he believes he is required to comply with this new law:

> The executive branch shall construe Title X in Division A of the Act, relating to detainees, in a manner consistent with the constitutional authority of the President to supervise the unitary executive branch and as Commander in Chief and consistent with the constitutional limitations on the judicial power, which will assist in achieving the shared objective of the Congress and the President, evidenced in Title X, of protecting the American people from further terrorist attacks.

In other words, the president will only apply the ban on torture "in a manner consistent with his constitutional authority." And as we have seen, the president's view of that authority is that such decisions "are for the President alone to make."

Here is what a January 4, 2006, article in *The Boston Globe* entitled "Bush Could Bypass New Torture Ban" reported:

> A senior administration official, who spoke to a Globe reporter about the statement on condition of anonymity because he is not an official spokesman, said the president intended to reserve the right

to use harsher methods in special situations involving national security. . . .

But, the official said, a situation could arise in which Bush may have to waive the law's restrictions to carry out his responsibilities to protect national security. He cited as an example a "ticking time bomb" scenario, in which a detainee is believed to have information that could prevent a planned terrorist attack.

"Of course the president has the obligation to follow this law, [but] he also has the obligation to defend and protect the country as the commander in chief, and he will have to square those two responsibilities in each case," the official added. "We are not expecting that those two responsibilities will come into conflict, but it's possible that they will."

Is it not extraordinary to see the U.S. Congress pass a hotly debated bill, one the president vigorously opposed and threatened to veto but finally signed into law, only to find out that the president "may have to waive the law's restrictions"? This law was enacted specifically to prohibit acts of torture the administration *has engaged in.* The American people, through their Congress, vigorously debated it. The president was rebuffed in his threat to veto it by the overwhelming support it received from the people's representatives in Congress. But democratic debate and voting don't matter, says the president, because he has the power to violate the law if he sees fit to do so.

The McCain torture ban is not the only law the president has expressly said, from the beginning, that he has the right to violate. The president applied the Yoo theory of presidential power in the form of a "signing statement" once again when the Congress, at the president's urging, renewed the PATRIOT Act. When Congress enacted the original PATRIOT Act in the aftermath of the 9/11 attacks, it inserted an expiration date of September 2005, at which point the law either had to be renewed or let expire. Congress voted to renew the law, with some modifications.

The new version granted—at the administration's request—highly controversial expanded police powers to the FBI. In order to calm public fears about these new powers, Congress required the president to report to Congress on how these new powers were used. But President Bush apparently decided that he did not want to abide by those new reporting provisions, and when he signed the bill into law on March 9, 2006, he again used his signing statement as a mechanism to assert his power to violate the law. As *The Boston Globe* reported on March 24, 2006:

> When President Bush signed the reauthorization of the USA PATRIOT Act this month, he included an addendum saying that he did not feel obliged to obey requirements that he inform Congress about how the FBI was using the act's expanded police powers.
>
> The bill contained several oversight provisions intended to make sure the FBI did not abuse the special terrorism-related powers to search homes and secretly seize papers. The provisions require Justice Department officials to keep closer track of how often the FBI uses the new powers and in what type of situations. Under the law, the administration would have to provide the information to Congress by certain dates.
>
> Bush signed the bill with fanfare at a White House ceremony March 9, calling it "a piece of legislation that's vital to win the war on terror and to protect the American people." But after the reporters and guests had left, the White House quietly issued a "signing statement," an official document in which a president lays out his interpretation of a new law.
>
> In the statement, Bush said that he did not consider himself bound to tell Congress how the PATRIOT Act powers were being used and that, despite the law's requirements, he could withhold the information if he decided that disclosure would "impair foreign relations, national security, the deliberative process of the executive, or the performance of the executive's constitutional duties."
>
> Bush wrote: "The executive branch shall construe the provisions . . . that call for furnishing information to entities outside the executive branch . . . in a manner consistent with the president's constitutional authority to supervise the unitary executive branch and to withhold information . . ."
>
> The statement represented the latest in a string of high-profile instances in which Bush has cited his constitutional authority to bypass a law.

This *Globe* article is an important milestone. It is one of the first truly comprehensive articles by an establishment media outlet to recognize the fact that the president has expressly seized the power to break the law and is exercising that power enthusiastically and aggressively, in numerous ways.

The series of controversies over the last five years involving radical and extreme government actions—from the use of torture to illegal eavesdropping to the lawless detention of U.S. citizens—cannot be viewed in isolation. They are but the symptoms—the ones we have learned about thus far—of a crisis in this country brought about by the fact that the president of the United States believes he has the power to act without restraint and to break the law.

That theory of lawlessness is evident in our government. We now have a governmental culture where violations of the law are literally the norm, and where theories have been adopted with the express purpose of claiming that the president is bestowed by the Constitution with the power to break the law. What we have in our federal government are not individual acts of lawbreaking or isolated scandals of illegality, but instead a culture and an ideology of lawlessness.

CHAPTER THREE

"What *Can't* He Do?"

The Weight of the Law

The NSA eavesdropping scandal, at its core, is not an eavesdropping scandal. It is a *lawbreaking* scandal, and it is unlike anything this country has confronted before.

Debates over the scope of executive power are not new. Throughout the nation's history, Americans have had passionate discussions about the value of a strong executive. But as the NSA scandal has illuminated so intensely, the Bush administration is not asserting that the country should have a "strong executive"; it is asserting that it should have an omnipotent ruler. The Bush administration does not argue that Congress has minimal powers in the areas of national security and terrorism; it argues that Congress has none. And these theories are most assuredly new for America.

As a result of the public controversy over this clear lawbreaking by the president, his defenders have been forced to argue unambiguously, and publicly, that they believe the president was justified in ordering illegal eavesdropping because he has the power to break the law when he deems that doing so is desirable for the security of the country.

The administration has never denied—because it cannot—that the eavesdropping the president ordered is exactly the kind that FISA prohibits. Almost immediately after disclosure of the warrantless eavesdropping program by *The New York Times,* Attorney General Alberto Gonzales appeared at a press briefing on December 19, 2005, to defend the president's decision to eavesdrop without judicial oversight:

> Now, in terms of legal authorities, the Foreign Intelligence Surveillance Act provides—requires a court order before engaging in this kind of surveillance that I've just discussed and the President announced on Saturday, unless there is somehow—there is—unless otherwise authorized by statute or by Congress. That's what the law requires.

While the attorney general thereafter advanced legal theories as to why the president had the right to engage in this eavesdropping without judicial approval, he admitted that, in the absence of a legal entitlement to act outside the law, FISA "requires a court order before engaging in this kind of surveillance." Instead, the administration has offered various and shifting legal justifications as to why the president had the right to engage in this eavesdropping without the judicial oversight required by that law.

From the moment the NSA surveillance program was first revealed, the administration has attacked FISA as a law that does not allow the president enough leeway in combatting terrorism. In his first press conference after disclosure of the illegal eavesdropping program, on December 19, 2005, President Bush claimed that the law does not grant enough of "an ability to move quickly to detect." Former NSA director General Michael Hayden echoed this claim at another press conference, on January 23, 2006, saying that FISA required too heavy a burden in order to obtain judicial approval for eavesdropping.

These complaints that FISA is too restrictive are groundless. FISA, after all, allows *immediate eavesdropping* for up to seventy-two hours when there is not enough time to obtain a warrant. Moreover, the FISA courts have *never* rejected a request by the government to eavesdrop. Ever since FISA was enacted in 1978, every president has complied with it and been able to aggressively defend the country.

Indeed, the FISA court operates like no other in the United States, precisely in order to ensure that immediate eavesdropping approval is always available. An article by James Bamford in the April 2006 *Atlantic Monthly* described some of the operational agility of the FISA court, with a focus on its longtime presiding judge, Reagan appointee Royce C. Lamberth:

> As the presiding justice of the Foreign Intelligence Surveillance Court, known as the FISA court, Lamberth had become accustomed to holding the secret hearings in his living room. . . . FBI agents will even knock on the judge's door in the middle of the night. "On the night of the bombings of the U.S. embassies in Africa, I started the first emergency hearings in my living room at 3:00 A.M.," recalled Lamberth. "From the outset, the FBI suspected bin Laden, and the surveillance I approved that night and in the ensuing days and weeks all ended up being critical evidence at the trial in New York."

The same article quotes Jonathan Turley, a George Washington University law professor who worked for the NSA as an intern in the 1980s: "I was shocked with what I saw. I was convinced that the [FISA] judge . . . would have signed anything that we put in front of him." Clearly, getting a warrant before eavesdropping on a potential terrorist is hardly cumbersome.

The administration's other principal excuse for eavesdropping in violation of FISA is one this country has heard before—and resoundingly rejected. President Richard Nixon's attorney general, John Mitchell, tried to calm Americans' fears in 1969 about the administration's power to eavesdrop in secret by telling them: "Any citizen of this United States who is not involved in some illegal activity has nothing to fear whatsoever." Similarly, President Bush's spokesman, Trent Duffy, told Americans on December 27, 2005, that there was no reason to worry about President Bush's warrantless eavesdropping because it is only used to "monitor calls from very bad people to very bad people."

But if, as the president claims, the administration is eavesdropping only on Al Qaeda members, or on Americans who are "very bad people," then it would be particularly easy to obtain judicial approval for this eavesdropping. No FISA judge has ever rejected a request to eavesdrop on an Al Qaeda member, and none ever would. If it is true, as the administration claims, that eavesdropping is directed only at those affiliated with terrorist groups, then there is really no conceivable reason why it would be necessary to eavesdrop without complying with FISA, since that is when it is the easiest to obtain judicial approval.

The complaints voiced by the administration about the supposed inadequacies of FISA—complaints it never voiced until the president was caught violating the law—are extremely difficult to understand, given how permissive and broad are the eavesdropping powers which the president has under the law. But this is the critical and often overlooked point: Even if the administration's complaints about the supposed inadequacies in the law were true, that could not possibly justify the president's lawbreaking. In a country under the rule of law, the solution to a bad or inadequate law is to change or amend the law—something that, in the case of FISA, could have been easily accomplished. The Congress repeatedly demonstrated that it was quite willing to expand the president's powers after the 9/11 attacks, and the president's own party controlled both houses of Congress for most of his tenure.

It defies credibility to claim that the president, in October 2001, ordered eavesdropping in violation of FISA because he perceived that the law imposed too many barriers to necessary eavesdropping. After all, he ordered this illegal eavesdropping at exactly the time, in October 2001, when Congress *was* amending FISA in accordance with the president's requests, and the president was telling the nation that, as a result of those amendments, he had all the tools he needed to monitor the communications of terrorists.

The president plainly broke the law, which is why the only defense available to him and his supporters is to claim that he has the right to do so.

In Defense of the President

For that reason, ever since the NSA scandal broke, the Bush administration has been forced to articulate its radical theories of presidential power out in the open. In the month after the scandal first emerged, numerous legal scholars, including many who are politically quite conservative, publicly criticized the president's conduct and emphatically argued that he broke the law. Numerous political officials and pundits from across the ideological spectrum did the same. Senators from the president's own party began demanding investigations, and normally pro-Bush political pundits were unwilling to endorse the notion that the president had the right to eavesdrop on Americans in violation of the law.

Unlike most political scandals, which burst into the media cycle with a fury only to quietly and inconsequentially fade away after a few days, the NSA eavesdropping scandal grew in intensity and seriousness. It was clear that many citizens of this country, for so long willing to give the president great leeway in the conduct of his office, were drawing a line at deliberate lawbreaking.

In response to that growing pressure, on January 19, 2006, the Department of Justice issued an unsigned, forty-two-page single-spaced letter entitled "Legal Authorities Supporting the Activities of the National Security Agency Described by the President," which set forth all of the administration's defenses against accusations that President Bush had violated the law. The letter did not deny that FISA bans warrantless eavesdropping. Instead, it simply offered legal justification for the president's right to act in violation of that law:

Because the President has determined that the NSA activities are necessary to the defense of the United States from a subsequent terrorist attack in the armed conflict with al Qaeda, FISA would impermissibly interfere with the President's most solemn constitutional obligation—to defend the United States against foreign attack.

That is the administration's truly extraordinary position in a nutshell. The Constitution not only allows but *requires* the president to defend the country. Therefore, the president is empowered to take any action he determines is "necessary to the defense of the United States from a subsequent terrorist attack," and any interference—whether from the law, the Congress, or the courts—is impermissible. And there is no recognition in any of the forty-two pages that there can be any limitations on George Bush's power. It is a naked theory of limitless presidential power. Among the highlights of the letter:

• The favorable citation of an argument made by Attorney General Black during the Civil War that statutes restricting the president's actions relating to war "could probably be read as simply providing 'a recommendation' that the president could decline to follow at his discretion" (p. 32).

• "The President's role as sole organ for the Nation in foreign affairs has long been recognized as carrying with it preeminent authority in the field of national security and foreign intelligence" (p. 30).

• "The President has independent authority to repel aggressive acts by third parties even without specific congressional authorization," and courts may not review the level of force selected (quoting a concurring opinion from appeals court Judge Laurence Silberman, long noted for his radical and fringe views on absolute executive power) (p. 10).

• The president's unlimited powers are not confined to being used abroad, but can be wielded "wherever [terrorists] may be—on United States soil or abroad."

Over and over, the Department of Justice letter depicts our government as vesting in the president full and unlimited authority to do anything—literally—he deems necessary to protect the nation against foreign threats. No formal war declaration by Congress is required. The president can exert these powers both inside the United States and against U.S. citizens. Congress cannot "interfere" with the president and the courts cannot review what he is doing.

All this leads directly to the question posed by former Vice President Al Gore when he gave a speech on January 16, 2006, to the Liberty Foundation, a speech that prominent conservative and former Republican congressman Bob Barr had agreed to introduce:

> Can it be true that any president really has such powers under our Constitution? If the answer is "yes," then under the theory by which these acts are committed, are there any acts that can on their face be prohibited? If the President has the inherent authority to eavesdrop, imprison citizens on his own declaration, kidnap and torture, *then what can't he do?*

The Bush administration has made its answer to this question as clear as possible: "Nothing."

Regarding the NSA program, since the Justice Department knows it cannot make a plausible argument that it complied with the requirements of FISA, the memorandum advocates theories that are about as far away as possible from the conservative legal principles Bush has always claimed to believe in and that he says he wants his judicial appointees to apply.

Thus, in addition to the claim that the president has unlimited powers under the Constitution, the Justice Department has also argued that the 2001 congressional resolution authorizing military force in Afghanistan and against Al Qaeda—a resolution that had nothing to do with FISA, eavesdropping, or surveillance, and never mentioned any of them—should nonetheless be "construed" and "interpreted" to have "impliedly" amended FISA by giving Bush an "exemption" entitling him to eavesdrop in violation of that law. This argument is made even though congressional leaders—including leading Republican senators such as Lindsey Graham of South Carolina, Arlen Specter of Pennsylvania, and Sam Brownback of Kansas—have said that it did no such thing.

Just how frivolous—and, for self-proclaimed judicial conservatives, hypocritical—this defense is can be seen in a different case, in which the Bush administration aggressively argued against the very legal theory it is now trying to peddle when it claims that Congress silently gave Bush an "exemption" to FISA. In a brief to the U.S. Supreme Court in the 2003 case *Breuer v. Jim's Concrete of Brevard*, signed by Bush's own solicitor general, Theodore Olson, the administration vehemently (and successfully) argued that a statute (such as FISA) *cannot* be "amended by implication" in the absence of clear congressional intent. The brief said in part:

> [T]he cardinal rule that repeals by implication are not favored, and will not be found unless an intent to repeal is clear and manifest. . . .
> In the absence of an affirmative showing of an intention to repeal, the only permissible justification for a repeal by implication is when the earlier and later statutes are irreconcilable. In other words, *where the two statutes are capable of co-existence, it is the duty of the courts, absent a clearly expressed congressional intention to the contrary, to regard each as effective.* [Emphasis added.]

Until George Bush needed an excuse for intentionally violating FISA, this was the administration's own argument: Congress cannot be said to have silently repealed its own law except when it subsequently passes a new law that is in direct conflict with the first one. What we really have from these paragons of judicial restraint is everything except plain language and original intent—the very tools of construction that these "conservatives," when not concocting legal defenses for the president, claim to believe in.

In order to defend Bush's illegal eavesdropping program, then, the administration is required to assert a position of presidential omnipotence. It has no choice. And its theory holds not merely that the president has the authority to break the law, but that he also has the authority to use *all war powers* against U.S. citizens on U.S. soil. The "war powers" a president can use in war against our enemies are virtually limitless—they include indefinite detention in prison with no charges or access to lawyers, limitless eavesdropping, and interrogation by means of torture.

In its January 19, 2006, defense of the president, the Justice Department actually argued that the president's powers include "at minimum, discretion to employ the traditional incidents of the use of military force" within the United States and against U.S. citizens (p. 10–11). The memo also said the president can use these powers "wherever [terrorists] may be—on United States soil or abroad." And these powers, in turn, "include all that is necessary and proper for carrying these powers into execution" (p. 7).

And not only do they have the right to use those war powers against Americans on U.S. soil, they have the right to use them even if Congress makes it a crime to do so or the courts rule that doing so is illegal. Put another way, the administration has now flatly stated that whatever it is allowed to do to our enemies, it can also do to our citizens, and that neither the Congress nor the courts can stop them.

Moreover, these theories apply not just to warrantless eavesdropping and indefinite imprisonment of U.S. citizens, but to a whole host of other draconian actions. To posit that the president can invoke war powers against U.S. citizens necessarily means that the president has the power to order physical searches of our homes without warrants, to open and read our mail without warrants, to declare martial law, even to order the torture or killing of citizens he deems to be "enemy combatants," just as long as he deems these actions necessary to defend the nation. Put simply, President Bush has seized the entire set of powers presidents have traditionally exercised in wartime, on the battlefield, against foreign enemies—but he claims the authority to exercise them, with no checks of any kind, against U.S. citizens on U.S. soil.

"A Strong, Robust Executive Authority"

To their credit, there are defenders of the administration who are nakedly honest about their view that the president should have no limits when using his "war powers." Vice President Dick Cheney, for one, told *The Washington Post* on December 20, 2005: "I believe in a strong, robust executive authority, and I think that the world we live in demands it—and to some extent that we have an obligation as the administration to pass on the offices we hold to our successors in as good of shape as we found them." In wartime, he told the newspaper, the president "needs to have his constitutional powers unimpaired."

And the elder Bush's attorney general, William Barr, admitted in the same article that he believes there are no limits on presidential power in "wartime"—which, of course, includes right now and will include, at a minimum, the remainder of Bush's term in office. "The Constitution's intent when we're under attack from outside is to place maximum power in the president," Barr told the *Post*, "and the other branches, and especially the courts, don't act as a check on the president's authority against the enemy."

It is true by definition that if—as Cheney and Barr claim—Congress and the courts don't "act as a check on the president's authority," then *nothing* does. Put simply, it is logically impossible for anyone who subscribes to this view to deny that they are advocating a monarchic president with unchecked powers.

Although Bush supporters frequently justify the assertion of these radical powers based on the principle that the United States is at war, there has never been a declaration of war under the Bush administration. Article I, Section 8, of the Constitution says flatly that "The Congress shall have Power . . . to declare war," but Congress has not done so under this administration. Congress has enacted resolutions authorizing the use of military force in places such as Afghanistan and Iraq, but that does not mean that the United States is "at war"—as Bush's own Attorney General, Alberto Gonzales, explained when he testified on February 6 before the Judiciary Committee:

> There was not a war declaration, either in connection with Al Qaida or in Iraq. It was an authorization to use military force. I only want to clarify that, because there are implications. Obviously, when you talk about a war declaration, you're possibly talking about affecting treaties, diplomatic relations. And so there is a distinction in law and in practice. And we're not talking about a war declaration. This is an authorization only to use military force.

And the undeclared "war" Bush supporters invoke in order to justify the president's seizure of unchecked powers is one that—by their own admission—they expect to last not a matter of years, but a matter of decades. It was revealed this year that the Defense Department has been referring to the effort to protect the country from terrorism as the "Long War." Ryan Henry, the Defense Department's deputy undersecretary for policy, explained in a February briefing why that term is used:

U.S. forces in all probability will be engaged somewhere in the world in the next decade where they're not currently engaged. But I can tell you with no resolution at all where that might be, when that might be or how that might be. Things get very fuzzy past the five-year point.

The president himself has repeatedly made clear that what he refers to as the war, which is what justifies his unlimited powers, certainly will not end during his administration, and likely not for several more decades.

As the scandals surrounding the president's lawbreaking have refused to disappear, the president's defenders have grown increasingly audacious and explicit about their real views of President Bush's power. The highly influential pro-Bush magazine *The Weekly Standard* published in its January 16, 2006, issue an extremely important essay by longtime social conservative hero Harvey Mansfield, a professor of government at Harvard. Entitled "The President and the Law," the article clearly sets forth the view of Bush defenders that as a result of the "war" we are fighting against terrorists, the president really is above the law, and the Constitution gives him the right to ignore both Congress and the courts:

> Enemies, however, not merely violate but oppose the law. They oppose our law and want to replace it with theirs. To counter enemies, a republic must have and use force adequate to a greater threat than comes from criminals, who may be quite patriotic if not public-spirited, and have nothing against the law when applied to others besides themselves. But enemies, being extra-legal, need to be faced with extra-legal force. . . .
>
> To confirm the extra-legal character of the presidency, the Constitution has him take an oath not to execute the laws but to execute the office of president, which is larger. . . .
>
> Yet the rule of law is not enough to run a government. Any set of standing rules is liable to encounter an emergency requiring an exception from the rule or an improvised response when no rule exists. In Machiavelli's terms, ordinary power needs to be supplemented or corrected by the extraordinary power of a prince, using wise discretion.
>
> In rejecting monarchy because it was unsafe, republicans had forgotten that it might also be effective. . . .

With one person in charge we can have both secrecy and responsibility. Here we have the reason that American society, in imitation of American government, makes so much use of one-man rule. . . .

Much present-day thinking puts civil liberties and the rule of law to the fore and forgets to consider emergencies when liberties are dangerous and law does not apply.

So, to recap: The president is "larger" than the law. The "rule of law is not enough to run a government." We must remember that a monarchy is "effective" and therefore, in times of "war," we must embrace "one-man rule." In sum, in emergencies like the one we have now and will have for the foreseeable future, the "*law does not apply.*"

That George Bush has the right to break the law is no longer a fringe, crackpot theory. This view is being expressly and unabashedly advocated in the most influential conservative magazine. It is endorsed by public intellectuals like Mansfield and by highly influential former officials like William Barr. Dick Cheney has made no bones about the fact that this is the administration's view, and of course, the Yoo memorandum long ago made clear that this "one-man rule" theory of executive power lies at the heart of the Bush administration.

CHAPTER FOUR

Patriotism Beyond Politics

The Right Hooks

Bruce Fein was a high-level Justice Department lawyer in the Reagan administration during the 1980s, a resident scholar with the right-wing Heritage Foundation, and a longtime outspoken advocate for conservative causes. There is nothing moderate about Fein's conservatism; he is a true believer in conservative principles. One illustration of his ideological bent came shortly after President George W. Bush's reelection, when he published an article in the February 2005 issue of *DC Bar* with some advice for the president regarding judicial appointments:

> President George W. Bush should pack the United States Supreme Court with philosophical clones of Justices Antonin Scalia and Clarence Thomas and defeated nominee Robert H. Bork. Multiple vacancies will inescapably arise in his second term. Senate Republicans should vote against the Senate filibuster rule as applied to thwart a floor vote for judicial nominees unconstitutional and unenforceable....
>
> A Supreme Court adhering to the Scalia-Thomas-Bork school of interpretation would strengthen democracy and the rule of law.

But ten months later, after *The New York Times* revealed on December 15, 2005, that President Bush had secretly ordered the NSA to eavesdrop on Americans in violation of FISA, Fein wrote a December 28 column in the right-wing newspaper *The Washington Times*, dismissing Bush's lawbreaking justifications as "nonsense" and proclaiming:

> Mr. Bush has adamantly refused to acknowledge any constitutional limitations on his power to wage war indefinitely against international terrorism, other than an unelaborated assertion he is not a dictator. Claims to inherent authority to break and enter homes, to

intercept purely domestic communications, or to herd citizens into concentration camps reminiscent of World War II, for example, have not been ruled out if the commander in chief believes the measures would help defeat Al Qaeda or sister terrorist threats.

Volumes of war powers nonsense have been assembled to defend Mr. Bush's defiance of the legislative branch and claim of wartime omnipotence so long as terrorism persists, i.e., in perpetuity. Congress should undertake a national inquest into his conduct and claims to determine whether impeachable usurpations are at hand....

Congress should insist the president cease the spying unless or until a proper statute is enacted or face possible impeachment. The Constitution's separation of powers is too important to be discarded in the name of expediency.

Objections to the president's lawbreaking have spanned the ideological spectrum. In fact, while many liberals and independents have vigorously opposed this patent lawbreaking, some of the harshest and most unyielding criticisms of the administration have come from highly conservative political figures such as Fein, who have eloquently and passionately argued that the powers claimed by President Bush constitute a profound assault on the most fundamental and defining American values.

The extremist theories that have taken hold in the executive branch for the last five years have nothing to do with liberal or conservative political ideology, nor do they have anything to do with being a Democrat or Republican. Rather, they are an outright betrayal of American values regarding government.

We are a nation of laws, where the people make the law. Our elected officials do not rule over us; they are our public servants. We cannot be imprisoned without charges and we have a right to be judged by a jury of our peers. Thus, when we enact legal restrictions through our Congress on what our government can do to us as citizens (as we did with FISA, or the ban on torture), those laws bind all citizens, including our elected officials.

Those are the values to which any American patriot, by definition, subscribes. Contrary to the central deceit manufactured by Bush defenders over the last five years, patriotism is not defined by loyalty to a particular elected official or political party. Indeed, excess loyalty to a single individual or party is the very antithesis of patriotism, as it places fealty to that individual or party over allegiance to the country, its interests, and its values. True patriotism is measured by the extent to which one believes in, and is willing to fight for and defend, the defining values and core principles of our country.

Opposition among conservatives to the administration's lawbreaking is substantial and growing, and it is easy to understand why. The administration's theories of presidential power trample on two of the bedrock conservative political principles—a restrained federal government and adherence to the rule of law. *Newsweek*'s Jonathan Alter described the developing rift on the ideological right:

> But "Snoopgate" is already creating new fissures on the right. The NSA story is an acid test of whether one is a traditional Barry Goldwater conservative, who believes in limited government, or a modern Richard Nixon conservative, who believes in authority.

This is exactly right. Longtime conservative journalist George Will, in his February 16, 2006, *Washington Post* column, wrote a scathing condemnation of the Bush administration's embrace of its "monarchical doctrine," and actually compared the dangers to our republic posed by the administration's abuses of power to the dangers posed by terrorists:

> Besides, terrorism is not the only new danger of this era. Another is the administration's argument that because the president is commander in chief, he is the "sole organ for the nation in foreign affairs." That non sequitur is refuted by the Constitution's plain language, which empowers Congress to ratify treaties, declare war, fund and regulate military forces, and make laws "necessary and proper" for the execution of all presidential powers. Those powers do not include deciding that a law—FISA, for example—is somehow exempted from the presidential duty to "take care that the laws be faithfully executed."

Will has adopted such a tone of urgency because he recognizes that the president is, with these theories, seizing the power to break the law:

This monarchical doctrine emerges from the administration's stance that warrantless surveillance by the National Security Agency targeting American citizens on American soil is a legal exercise of the president's inherent powers as commander in chief, even though it violates the clear language of the 1978 Foreign Intelligence Surveillance Act, which was written to regulate wartime surveillance.

Like Fein's, Will's criticism of the president's claim to be above the law is undiluted and unapologetic, because his principal allegiance is to the defining values of our country—values that transcend liberalism or conservatism and that are vastly more important than partisan political interests.

Few political figures can match the conservative credentials of former congressman Bob Barr of Georgia. He was the primary sponsor of the Defense of Marriage Act of 1996, which banned the recognition by the federal government of gay marriages. He was a House manager of the impeachment proceedings against Bill Clinton, and one of the driving forces behind it. He is on the National Rifle Association board, and had one of the most conservative voting records in the country during his eight years in Congress.

On December 16, 2005—the day after the *Times* first revealed the NSA lawbreaking—Barr appeared on CNN with Wolf Blitzer, along with Bush defender Rep. Dana Rohrabacher. Here is Barr's response when Blitzer asked him, "What's wrong with what the President has decided to do?"

> What's wrong with it is several-fold. One, it's bad policy for our government to be spying on American citizens through the National Security Agency. Secondly, it's bad to be spying on Americans without court oversight. And thirdly, it's bad to be spying on Americans apparently in violation of federal laws against doing it without court order. So it's bad all around, and we need to get to the bottom of this.

When Rohrabacher began offering justifications as to why the president achieved good results by violating the law, Barr was outraged:

Well, the fact of the matter is that the Constitution is the Constitution, and I took an oath to abide by it. My good friend, my former colleague, Dana Rohrabacher, did and the president did. And I don't really care very much whether or not it can be justified based on some hypothetical. The fact of the matter is that, if you have any government official who deliberately orders that federal law be violated despite the best of motives, that certainly ought to be of concern to us. . . .

Here again, this is absolutely a bizarre conversation where you have a member of Congress saying that it's okay for the president of the United States to ignore U.S. law, to ignore the Constitution, simply because we are in an undeclared war. The fact of the matter is the law prohibits—specifically prohibits—what apparently was done in this case, and for a member of Congress to say, 'Oh, that doesn't matter, I'm proud that the president violated the law' is absolutely astounding, Wolf.

As is clear from the reactions of conservatives like Fein and Will and Barr, the Bush doctrine of unchecked presidential power is neither conservative nor liberal. It can only be described as radical and extremist, precisely because it finds no home, and no support, in either liberal or conservative ideology.

Conservatives and liberals rarely agree on controversial issues, and when they do, it is because, as Americans, they share a set of fundamental values and beliefs. It is those values that are under assault by the Bush administration, and by resisting that assault, one is defending neither conservative nor liberal political views. One is defending core American values.

All-American Blogosphere

On February 20, 2006, the British historian David Irving was sentenced by an Austrian criminal court to three years in prison for violations of an Austrian law that criminally punishes "whoever denies, grossly plays down, approves or tries to excuse the National Socialist genocide or other National Socialist crimes against humanity in a print publication, in broadcast or other media." Irving had been wanted in Austria as a result of two 1989 speeches in which he denied that six million Jews had been exterminated in the Holocaust. In sum, Irving was convicted and impris-oned for expressing ideas the Austrian government has banned.

Although this story received very little attention from the U.S. media, it was widely discussed in the "blogosphere." And that discussion illus-trates an extremely important point about what is meant when one refers to "core American values."

I created my own political blog, Unclaimed Territory, in October 2005, and I had been actively reading numerous blogs from across the political spectrum for roughly two years prior to that. As polarized as our national political dialogue is, the blogosphere is far more polarized. Vir-tually every blog is firmly entrenched on either the Right or the Left, and almost every news event, large and small, breeds vehement disagreement.

But the conviction and sentencing of David Irving was one news event where bloggers who normally cannot agree on the time of day were expressing the same opinions and advocating the same ideals. Virtually every American blogger who wrote about it—from the most liberal to the most conservative—was in complete agreement regarding the impropri-ety of Irving's punishment. They all unambiguously expressed the opin-ion that while those who deny or downplay the Holocaust are deplorable, nobody should be imprisoned or prosecuted by the state for expressing an idea, no matter how repugnant it might be.

The agreement was as complete as it was rare. Liberal blogger Shake-speare's Sister wrote: "I certainly don't want this to be read as some sort of deranged apologia for Holocaust deniers, because that's not remotely what I intend. They're scum. I'm just wondering, even though Holocaust denial is enormously offensive, why it is criminal." Conservative blogger Mark Coffey of the Decision '08 blog pointedly opined: "Yeah, he's a scum-bag, but he ought to be free to be a scumbag." Another conservative blog-ger, Bill Quick of Daily Pundit, opined somewhat more eloquently: "It's a truism because it is true: if unpopular views enjoy no rights to free expres-sion, no views do. The right does not exist, or, rather, it exists, but is ignored." And liberal blogger Roger Ailes, after excoriating Irving, acknowledged: "I'd oppose the criminal law on principle."

That sort of transpartisan ideological consensus is almost unheard of these days with regard to any issue, and it raises several extremely interest-ing and important points regarding what it means to be American.

There is a set of fundamental political values that Americans have ingrained within them by virtue of growing up in this country, being educated here, and being inculcated with common perceptions of the country's founding and its history. (By "political values" I mean that the values pertain to principles of government and law, rather than to, say, personal conduct or private morality.) And when immigration policies are managed correctly, immigrants arrive here with those values already incubated or with an instinctive openness to them (which is one of the reasons they want to come here), and they come eventually to embrace these values as well, regardless of political ideology.

One ingrained American political principle is that citizens cannot and must not be punished by the state for expressing ideas and opinions, no matter how reprehensible, repulsive, or even dangerous those ideas and opinions may be. That is a founding and defining principle of America; it is one of the ideals that make America America. It is a principle guaranteed by the First Amendment to the U.S. Constitution, which dictates that "Congress shall make no law . . . abridging the freedom of speech," and it cannot be characterized or understood as a "liberal" or "conservative" belief. It transcends ideology and contemporary partisan conflicts. It is a core *American* value.

It is this set of transcendent political values on which opposition to George Bush's violations of the law and radical theories of power is predicated. Just as Americans cannot be punished by the government for expressing their opinions, neither can they be imprisoned by their government without due process, that is, without their proverbial day in court. All Americans are equal under the law, and in America nobody, including the president, is above the law or exempt from its mandates. Governmental power in America always emanates from the people, such that Americans have the right to enact laws through their representatives in Congress, and nobody—including the president—has the right to violate those laws.

These are the principles that led Americans in 1978 to enact a law, in response to decades of eavesdropping abuses by administrations of both parties, that made it a criminal offense for our government to eavesdrop on Americans without judicial oversight and approval. It was neither a conservative nor a liberal belief—as evidenced by the fact that the United

States Senate approved FISA in 1978 by a vote of 95 to 1. Those representatives voted as one because a consensus had been reached democratically that reflected the will of the people.

These are the principles at stake here, and they are not even remotely ideological ones. None of this is about eavesdropping or FISA or Al Qaeda or liberalism or conservatism. Like the David Irving conviction, the controversy surrounding the administration's radical theories of power is about the principles of government on which our country was founded and which most Americans, by definition, instinctively embrace, regardless of political ideology.

Revolutionary Wisdom

The founders of our country were willing to risk their lives—literally—to fight a war against the most powerful empire on earth, precisely because they did not want to live under a system of government where a ruler could assert unlimited powers, including the power to break the law, to search them without warrants, or to imprison them without a trial. The American Revolution was born of a refusal to live under a ruler who could override the will of the majority, exercise tyrannical powers, and generally rule without checks or restraints.

The founders drafted a Constitution that is carefully crafted so all three branches of government are co-equal and serve as a check on the other two. The division of power among the branches of government mandated by the Constitution could not be clearer. Article I vests the power to make the law exclusively in the American people, through their representatives in Congress: "All legislative Powers herein granted shall be vested in a Congress of the United States, which shall consist of a Senate and House of Representatives." The power to interpret those laws is vested in the courts by Article III: "The judicial Power of the United States, shall be vested in one supreme Court, and in such inferior Courts as the Congress may from time to time ordain and establish."

The president possesses the power neither to make laws nor to interpret them. And it ought to go without saying that he does not possess the power to ignore laws or to break them. Instead, the role of the president, as set forth by Article II, is to implement and enforce the laws enacted by the people through their Congress: "He shall take Care that the Laws be faithfully executed."

These constitutional principles are also enumerated in the Federalist Papers, a series of arguments written by James Madison, Alexander Hamilton, and John Jay, which were designed to educate the colonists about the virtues of the federal Constitution and to persuade them to adopt it.

Just how repellent to our founding principles is the Bush administration's assertion of unchecked presidential power—in particular the claim that decisions relating to terrorism and national security "are for the President alone to make"—is conclusively demonstrated by James Madison's Federalist No. 48, which warns that liberty cannot be maintained unless each branch remains accountable and subordinate to the others:

> It was shown in the last paper that the political apothegm there examined does not require that the legislative, executive, and judiciary departments should be wholly unconnected with each other. I shall undertake, in the next place, to show that unless these departments be so far connected and blended as to give to each a constitutional control over the others, the degree of separation which the maxim requires, as essential to a free government, can never in practice be duly maintained.

Similarly, in Federalist No. 51 Madison defines the central method of avoiding tyranny as ensuring that no branch of government—or "department"—be able to claim for itself powers which are absolute and unchecked by the other branches:

> What expedient, then, shall we finally resort, for maintaining in practice the necessary partition of power among the several departments, as laid down in the Constitution? The only answer that can be given is, that as all these exterior provisions are found to be inadequate, the defect must be supplied, by so contriving the interior structure of the government as that its several constituent parts may, by their mutual relations, be the means of keeping each other in their proper places. . . .

While each branch of government must be restrained by the other two, the founders insisted that all government power derives ultimately from the people, which meant that instrument of the people's will—the Congress and the laws it enacted—would predominate. In particular, Madison emphasized in Federalist No. 51 that liberty could be preserved only if the laws enacted by the people through the Congress were supreme and universally binding:

> But it is not possible to give to each department an equal power of self-defense. In republican government, the legislative authority necessarily predominates.

Hamilton made the same point in Federalist No. 73, where he emphasized "the superior weight and influence of the legislative body in a free government, and the hazard to the Executive in a trial of strength with that body. . . ."

The notion that the most significant and consequential decisions for our nation are "for the President alone to make" is precisely what the Founders warned against. Here is Madison in Federalist No. 58:

> An elective despotism was not the government we fought for; but one in which the powers of government should be so divided and balanced among the several bodies of magistracy as that no one could transcend their legal limits without being effectually checked and restrained by the others.

It also cannot be said that the founders were unaware of the potential for national emergencies and external threats. They engaged in a war with Britain, then the most powerful country on earth. This was a much graver threat to the republic than that posed by 9/11 and Islamic terrorism. If the Revolutionary War had been lost, there would have been no America.

To the founders, the defining characteristics of the tyrannical British king was that he possessed precisely those powers that the Constitution prohibits but the Bush administration is now claiming it can exercise. From Federalist No. 70:

In England, the king is a perpetual magistrate; and it is a maxim which has obtained for the sake of the public peace, that he is unaccountable for his administration, and his person sacred.

The notion that the president has the right to act in violation of duly enacted laws would have been repellent to all of the founders, including the great American revolutionary Thomas Paine, who wrote in his legendary 1776 pamphlet *Common Sense* that those who claim the power President Bush is claiming—namely, to act in violation of the law—are claiming the power of a king:

But where says some is the King of America? I'll tell you Friend, he reigns above, and doth not make havoc of mankind like the Royal Brute of Britain. . . . Let it be brought forth placed on the divine law, the word of God; let a crown be placed thereon, by which the world may know, that so far as we approve of monarchy, that in America THE LAW IS KING.

Based on the fear of such unchecked executive power, Federalist No. 69 emphasized that unlike the British king, who did possess the absolute power to nullify duly enacted laws, the *sole power* possessed by the president to negate a law enacted by Congress—even relating to matters of national security and war—is the president's qualified (i.e., overrideable) veto power:

Hence it appears that, except as to the concurrent authority of the President in the article of treaties, it would be difficult to determine whether that magistrate would, in the aggregate, possess more or less power than the Governor of New York. And it appears yet more unequivocally, that there is no pretense for the parallel which has been attempted between him and the king of Great Britain. . . .

The one [the American president] would have a qualified negative upon the acts of the legislative body; the other [the British king] has an absolute negative. The one would have a right to command the military and naval forces of the nation; the other, in addition to this right, possesses that of declaring war, and of raising and regulating fleets and armies by his own authority.

An extremely potent demonstration that the Bush administration's claim to unchecked executive power is fundamentally inconsistent with the most basic constitutional safeguards comes from one of the unlikeliest corners—Justice Antonin Scalia's opinion in *Hamdi v. Rumsfeld* in 2004, where Scalia explained that in the area of national security, even in times of war, the president's power as commander in chief is limited to tactical decisions about how the country's armies will fight:

> The proposition that the Executive lacks indefinite wartime detention authority over citizens is consistent with the Founders' general mistrust of military power permanently at the Executive's disposal. In the Founders' view, the "blessings of liberty" were threatened by "those military establishments which must gradually poison its very fountain." The Federalist No. 45, p. 238 (J. Madison). No fewer than 10 issues of the Federalist were devoted in whole or part to allaying fears of oppression from the proposed Constitution's authorization of standing armies in peacetime.
>
> Many safeguards in the Constitution reflect these concerns. Congress's authority "[t]o raise and support Armies" was hedged with the proviso that "no Appropriation of Money to that Use shall be for a longer Term than two Years." U. S. Const., Art. 1, §8, cl. 12. Except for the actual command of military forces, all authorization for their maintenance and all explicit authorization for their use is placed in the control of Congress under Article I, rather than the President under Article II.
>
> As Hamilton explained, the president's military authority would be "much inferior" to that of the British King: "It would amount to nothing more than the supreme command and direction of the military and naval forces, as first general and admiral of the confederacy: while that of the British king extends to the *declaring* of war, and to the *raising* and *regulating* of fleets and armies; all which, by the constitution under consideration, would appertain to the legislature." The Federalist No. 69, p. 357.
>
> A view of the Constitution that gives the executive authority to use military force rather than the force of law against citizens on American soil flies in the face of the mistrust that engendered these provisions.

It is difficult to overstate the importance of these observations from Justice Scalia, the favorite Supreme Court justice of conservatives, the man whom President Bush himself identified during his reelection campaign as an ideal justice. The United States Constitution applies in both peacetime and war, and even in war the power of the president is subject to checks and balances by Congress and the courts, and his power is limited to command of the armed forces. There is no time in America—whether in peace or at war—when the president has the powers that the Bush administration has attempted to seize.

Moreover, while President Bush's supporters are fond of referring to him as the "commander in chief"—typically to insinuate that he should be beyond criticism or that his authority cannot be questioned, particularly in "times of war"—the president under our system of government holds that position only with regard to those in the armed forces (see Article II, Section 2 of the Constitution: "The president shall be Commander in Chief of the Army and Navy of the United States"). With regard to Americans generally, the president is not our "commander" but instead our elected public servant, subject to the mandates of the law like every other citizen and subordinate to the will of the people.

Critically, as Justice Scalia points out, even in wartime, the president's powers as commander in chief are extremely narrow and limited. As Hamilton put it, "It would amount to nothing more than the supreme command and direction of the military and naval forces."

The founders of our country understood as well as anyone the exigencies of war and anticipated that the country would likely be at war in the future. They specifically and expressly limited the powers of the president as commander in chief both during peace and during wartime, and they provided no wartime exceptions to any of the limitations placed by the Constitution on the power of the president.

The Youngstown *Decision*

In 1952, in the midst of the Korean War, American steelworkers decided they would go on a nationwide strike, which President Harry S Truman believed—accurately—would result in a steel shortage that would seriously affect U.S. national security. To avert that devastating problem,

Truman wanted to seize the steel factories and use them to continue to produce steel. He had previously asked Congress to enact legislation giving him this seizure power, but Congress refused, instead enacting legislation that gave the president some new powers to deal with problems posed by such strikes but did not include the power to seize factories.

Unlike George Bush—who, in the case of FISA, simply violated the law in secret—the Truman administration argued its position in the federal courts. It had the right to seize the factories, it claimed, and it asked the Supreme Court to rule that the president had the "inherent authority" under the Constitution to do so—even though Congress had refused to give him this power. In *Youngstown Co. v. Sawyer*, the Supreme Court resoundingly rejected the Truman administration's assertions. Just as the Bush administration is doing now, the Truman administration then argued that national security required the president to exercise his inherent authority in violation of congressional will. As the Supreme Court in *Youngstown* explained:

> Opposing the motion for preliminary [343 U.S. 579, 584] injunction, the United States asserted that a strike disrupting steel production for even a brief period would so endanger the well-being and safety of the Nation that the President had "inherent power" to do what he had done—power "supported by the Constitution, by historical precedent, and by court decisions."

Just as the Bush administration has with regard to FISA, the Truman administration then claimed that the law passed by Congress to address the problem was inadequate and too time-consuming to deal with the threats. From *Youngstown*:

> The Government refers to the seizure provisions of one of these statutes (201 (b) of the Defense Production Act) as "much too cumbersome, involved, and time-consuming for the crisis which was at hand."

The Supreme Court unequivocally rejected these arguments—because under the Constitution, it is the Congress that makes the laws, and the president must abide by them. The Court explained:

The Constitution limits his functions in the lawmaking process to the recommending of laws he thinks wise and the vetoing of laws he thinks bad. And the Constitution is neither silent nor equivocal about who shall make laws which the President is to execute. The [343 U.S. 579, 588] first section of the first article says that "All legislative Powers herein granted shall be vested in a Congress of the United States . . . ."

The Founders of this Nation entrusted the lawmaking power to the Congress alone in both good and bad times. It would do no good to recall the historical events, the fears of power and the hopes for freedom that lay behind their choice. Such a review would but confirm our holding that this seizure order cannot stand.

The concurring opinions by justices Felix Frankfurter, William Douglas, and Robert Jackson elaborated on the rationale behind that opinion. First, Justice Frankfurter explained that the founders insisted upon limitations on the president's power *even in times of emergency,* because the risk of autocracy was greater than the risk that such limitations would impair our security:

> A scheme of government like ours no doubt at times feels the lack of power to act with complete, all-embracing, swiftly moving authority. No doubt a government with distributed authority, subject to be challenged in the courts of law, at least long enough to consider and adjudicate the challenge, labors under restrictions from which other governments are free. It has not been our tradition to envy such governments. In any event our government was designed to have such restrictions. The price was deemed not too high in view of the safeguards which these restrictions afford. I know no more impressive words on this subject than those of Mr. Justice Brandeis:
>> "The doctrine of the separation of powers was adopted by the Convention of 1787, not to promote efficiency but to preclude the exercise of arbitrary power. The purpose was, not to avoid friction, but, [343 U.S. 579, 614] by means of the inevitable friction incident to the distribution of the

governmental powers among three departments, to save
the people from autocracy."

Justice Douglas emphasized the supremacy of the rule of law—as
enacted by Congress—which lies at the heart of our system of government:

> The power to recommend legislation, granted to the President,
> serves only to emphasize that it is his function to recommend and
> that it is the function of the Congress to legislate. Article II, [343 U.S.
> 579, 633] Section 3 also provides that the President "shall take Care
> that the Laws be faithfully executed." But, as MR. JUSTICE BLACK
> and MR. JUSTICE FRANKFURTER point out, *the power to execute
> the laws starts and ends with the laws Congress has enacted.* [Empha-
> sis added.]

And in a concurring opinion that ought to be read by every defender of
President Bush's claim to unchecked power—a concurring opinion that
most legal scholars, including recent Bush Supreme Court appointee
Samuel Alito, agree is the governing framework for analyzing the limits of
executive power—Justice Jackson made clear just how incompatible with
our republic are theories that give the president the right to act in violation of congressional statutes:

> The Solicitor General seeks the power of seizure in three clauses of
> the Executive Article, the first reading, "The executive Power shall be
> vested in a President of the United States of America." Lest I be
> thought to exaggerate, I quote the interpretation which his brief puts
> upon it: "In our view, this clause constitutes a grant of all the execu-
> tive powers of which the Government is capable." If that be true, it
> is difficult to see why the [343 U.S. 579, 641] forefathers bothered to
> add several specific items, including some trifling ones.
>
> The example of such unlimited executive power that must have
> most impressed the forefathers was the prerogative exercised by
> George III, and the description of its evils in the Declaration of Inde-
> pendence leads me to doubt that they were creating their new Exec-
> utive in his image.

As Justice Jackson points out, the notion that a president can disregard and violate laws when he deems it to be in the national interest is precisely one of the powers exercised by King George III that spawned the American Revolution.

Finally, Justice Jackson demolishes the claim that the exigencies of "war"—especially undeclared wars, like the one the Bush administration claims the country is now fighting—allow the president to claim the right to act in violation of congressional laws based on claimed inherent executive authority:

> Thus, it is said, he has invested himself with "war powers."
>
> I cannot foresee all that it might entail if the Court should endorse this argument. Nothing in our Constitution is plainer than that declaration of a war is entrusted only to Congress. Of course, a state of war may in fact exist without a formal declaration. But no doctrine that the Court could promulgate would seem to me more sinister and alarming than that a President whose conduct of foreign affairs is so largely uncontrolled, and often even is unknown, can vastly enlarge his mastery over the internal affairs of the country by his own commitment of the Nation's armed forces to some foreign venture. 10 [343 U.S. 579, 643] . . . .
>
> The appeal, however, that we declare the existence of inherent powers *ex necessitate* to meet an emergency asks us to do what many think would be wise, although [343 U.S. 579, 650] it is something the forefathers omitted. They knew what emergencies were, knew the pressures they engender for authoritative action, knew, too, how they afford a ready pretext for usurpation.
>
> We may also suspect that they suspected that emergency powers would tend to kindle emergencies. Aside from suspension of the privilege of the writ of habeas corpus in time of rebellion or invasion, when the public safety may require it, they made no express provision for exercise of extraordinary authority because of a crisis. I do not think we rightfully may so amend their work, and, if we could, I am not convinced it would be wise to do so, although many modern nations have forthrightly recognized that war and economic crises may upset the normal balance between liberty and authority. [343 U.S. 579, 651]

Their experience with emergency powers may not be irrelevant to the argument here that we should say that the Executive, of his own volition, can invest himself with undefined emergency powers.

The arguments President Bush's defenders are trying to use to justify his violations of the law have all been considered—and decisively rejected—by the Supreme Court. The Court made clear that a country that lives under the rule of law cannot tolerate a president who asserts the power to act contrary to the laws enacted by the people through their Congress. The Supreme Court in *Youngstown* reaffirmed the basic principle of our government: that the rule of law is supreme and the president has no power to violate duly enacted congressional laws, no matter his claimed justifications.

"Oppressive and Lawless"

What is at risk from the Bush administration's radical theories of power are not new or exotic liberties, but rather the most fundamental rights. The right the Bush administration denied to U.S. citizens Padilla and Hamdi—that is, the right not to be imprisoned without due process—is a right that was not just recognized at the founding of the country, but was one of the first liberties established in thirteenth-century England, when British subjects rejected the notion that the king had absolute, unlimited powers and forced King John to accept the Magna Carta. That thirteenth-century liberty is what has been abrogated by this administration. As Justice Jackson wrote in his concurring opinion in the 1953 case of *Brown v. Allen*:

> Executive imprisonment has been considered oppressive and lawless since John, at Runnymede, pledged that no free man should be imprisoned, dispossessed, outlawed, or exiled save by the judgment of his peers or by the law of the land. The judges of England developed the writ of habeas corpus largely to preserve these immunities from executive restraint.

And the very notion that the president can order a U.S. citizen imprisoned with no review, or that the president can decide for himself which laws to enforce and how they will be enforced, was the greatest danger Madison warned about. As he put it with perfect prescience in Federalist No. 47:

> From these facts, by which Montesquieu was guided, it may clearly be inferred that, in saying "There can be no liberty where the legislative and executive powers are united in the same person, or body of magistrates," or, "if the power of judging be not separated from the legislative and executive powers," he did not mean that these departments ought to have no partial agency in, or no control over, the acts of each other.
>
> His meaning, as his own words import, and still more conclusively as illustrated by the example in his eye, can amount to no more than this, that where the whole power of one department is exercised by the same hands which possess the whole power of another department, the fundamental principles of a free constitution are subverted. This would have been the case in the constitution examined by him, if the king, who is the sole executive magistrate, had possessed also the complete legislative power, or the supreme administration of justice; or if the entire legislative body had possessed the supreme judiciary, or the supreme executive authority.

And while it is the case that some of the liberties protected by the U.S. Constitution were vigorously debated and subject to all sorts of compromises among the founders, the right not to be imprisoned by the federal government without due process was not one of those controversies.

It was indisputably clear to the founders that liberty cannot exist if the government is empowered to imprison its citizens without charging them with a crime, without allowing them the opportunity to defend themselves against the crime, and without the government having to prove that they committed a crime. Thomas Jefferson wrote in a 1789 letter to Thomas Paine: "I consider [trial by jury] as the only anchor ever yet imagined by man, by which a government can be held to the principles of its constitution."

Disputes over constitutional liberties are often characterized by esoteric and abstract arguments that only constitutional lawyers can really decipher. That is not the case for the right not to be imprisoned by George Bush without a trial. The rights provided by the founders that protect us from such treatment could not be clearer, and require no debate. The Fifth Amendment provides:

> No person shall be held to answer for a capital, or otherwise infamous crime, unless on a presentment or indictment of a Grand Jury ... nor shall be compelled in any criminal case to be a witness against himself, nor be deprived of life, liberty, or property, without due process of law.

And the Sixth Amendment guarantees that "in all criminal prosecutions, the accused shall . . . be informed of the nature and cause of the accusation." The powers the Bush administration has now seized for itself—specific powers such as the ability to listen to all of our communications without safeguards or oversight, or to arrest and detain us with no trial—are powers that could not be more antithetical to the principles on which our country was based.

Nor can any of these excesses be justified by constant warnings about the evils of terrorism, or strident speeches endlessly emphasizing the dangers we face as a nation. Throughout its history, the United States has faced all manner of external threats and dangerous enemies. The founders knew full well that America would have foreign enemies and would likely fight future wars. After all, they had just fought one. But they nonetheless argued that such threats do not justify a departure from the principles of government that keep us free and prevent tyranny.

To the contrary, they warned us that tyrants and despots—those who would seek to seize power beyond what our Constitution allows—would be easily recognizable by their attempted exploitation of fear, and their promises of protection, all in order to justify abridgments of our liberties and to persuade us to accept their seizures of unchecked power in exchange for being "safe."

America has emerged as the world's strongest country not despite but *because of* the limitations on government power that our Constitution imposes. We are a strong nation precisely because we have adhered to our founding principles of liberty and a restrained government, not because we have departed from them in times of danger or due to fear.

The arguments invoked by the Bush administration to justify its seizure of unlimited power—that our security and safety require us to entrust those powers to the president—are exactly the ones the founders repeatedly warned us would be used by those seeking to subvert our constitutional democracy.

CHAPTER FIVE

Fear as a Weapon

Be Very Afraid

In one sense, it is difficult to understand how the Bush administration has been able to embrace such radical theories of executive power, and to engage in such recognizably un-American conduct—first in the shadows and now quite openly—without prompting a far more intense backlash from the country than we have seen. It is true that the president's approval ratings have sunk to new lows in 2005 and 2006. The broad and bipartisan support he commanded for the two years after the 9/11 attacks has vanished almost completely. And yet, despite all of the public opinion trends and the president's steadily declining popularity, there has been no resounding public rejection of the administration's claim to virtually limitless executive power and its systematic violations of the nation's laws.

That is because the Bush administration has in its arsenal one very potent weapon—and one weapon only—which it has repeatedly used: fear. Ever since September 11, 2001, Americans have been bombarded with warnings, with color-coded "alerts," with talk of mushroom clouds and nefarious plots to blow up bridges and tall buildings, with villains assigned cartoon names such as "dirty bomber," "Dr. Germ," and so on. And there has been a constant barrage from the White House of impending threats that generate fear—fear of terrorism, fear of more 9/11–style attacks, fear of nuclear annihilation, fear of our ports being attacked, fear of our water systems being poisoned—and, of course, fear of excessive civil liberties or cumbersome laws jeopardizing our "homeland security."

Our very survival is at risk, we are told. We face an enemy unlike any we have seen before, more powerful than anything we have previously encountered. President Bush is devoted to protecting us from the terrorists. We have to invade and occupy Iraq because the terrorists will kill us all if we do not. We must allow the president to incarcerate American citizens without due process, employ torture as a state-sanctioned weapon, eavesdrop on our private conversations, and even violate the law, because the terrorists are so evil and so dangerous that we cannot have any limits on the power of the president if we want him to protect us from the dangers in the world.

That terrorism is a real and serious threat cannot be denied. But America has never been a nation characterized by fear. Yet, for the last five years, we have had a government that has worked overtime to keep fear levels high because doing so served its interests. More than four years after the 9/11 attacks, the Bush administration continues to keep up the relentless drumbeat of fear. Here is Dick Cheney in early January 2006, proudly defending the administration's illegal eavesdropping program by invoking the specter of terrorism fears:

> As we get farther away from September 11th, some in Washington are yielding to the temptation to downplay the ongoing threat to our country, and to back away from the business at hand....
>
> The enemy that struck on 9/11 is weakened and fractured, yet it is still lethal and trying to hit us again. Either we are serious about fighting this war or we are not. And as long as George W. Bush is President of the United States, we are serious—and we will not let down our guard.

Cheney never once addresses the fact that the administration had full leeway to eavesdrop on terrorists without breaking the law. He ignores that fact because he is not making a rational argument. He is attempting to play on the fears of Americans to justify their violations of law.

President Bush has also been fueling the fires of fear in almost every speech he has given since September 11, 2001. Here he is in a typical speech, delivered on October 6, 2005, transparently attempting to whip up as much fear as possible in order to try to prop up Americans' diminishing support for the country's ongoing occupation of Iraq:

> The militants believe that controlling one country will rally the Muslim masses, enabling them to overthrow all moderate governments in the region, and establish a radical Islamic empire that spans from Spain to Indonesia. With greater economic and military and political power, the terrorists would be able to advance their stated agenda: to develop weapons of mass destruction, to destroy Israel, to

intimidate Europe, to assault the American people, and to blackmail our government into isolation.

Our enemy is utterly committed. As Zarqawi has vowed, "We will either achieve victory over the human race or we will pass to the eternal life." And the civilized world knows very well that other fanatics in history, from Hitler to Stalin to Pol Pot, consumed whole nations in war and genocide before leaving the stage of history. . . .

With the rise of a deadly enemy and the unfolding of a global ideological struggle, our time in history will be remembered for new challenges and unprecedented dangers.

Islamic terrorists, here as always, are depicted as omnipotent villains with quite attainable dreams of world domination, genocide, and the obliteration of the United States. They are trying to take over the world and murder us all. And this is not merely a threat we face. It is much more than that. It is *the predominant issue* facing the United States—more important than all others. Everything pales in comparison to fighting off this danger. We face not merely a danger, but "unprecedented dangers."

For four years, this is what Americans have heard over and over and over from our government—that we face a mortal and incomparably powerful enemy, and only the most extreme measures taken by our government can save us. We are a nation engaged in a War of Civilizations, a nation whose very existence is in peril. All of our plans for the future, dreams for our children, career aspirations, life goals—these are all subordinate, all for naught, unless, first and foremost, we stand loyally behind George Bush as he takes the extreme and unprecedented measures necessary to protect us from these extreme and unprecedented threats.

It is that deeply irrational, fear-driven view of the world that has been used to convince Americans to acquiesce to the administration's excesses and abuses of power. And it is not difficult to understand why it works.

After all, if it really were the case that terrorism constituted the sort of imminent, civilization-ending threat the administration has spent the last four years drumming into everyone's head, then it might be extremely difficult to gin up much outrage over an eavesdropping program—warrants or not—or over a few American citizens being rounded up and put in military prisons without any charges. When our very survival is in imminent danger, all else pales in importance, and we may feel extreme gratitude toward those who seek to save us, even if they break a few laws to do it.

In fact, it has become unacceptable in polite company to even raise the prospect that the threat of terrorism may be exaggerated. During the 2004 election, John Kerry stumbled in his clumsy way towards challenging this fear-mongering when he was quoted in *The New York Times Magazine* as saying, "We have to get back to the place we were, where terrorists are not the focus of our lives, but they're a nuisance." This provoked the predictable outrage from the Bush camp that Kerry, along with Bush's other opponents, was not serious about fighting terrorists and was too weak to protect our children from this unparalleled menace, and the issue was never spoken of again.

It has become an inviolable piety that there is no such thing as overstating the terrorism risk. One is compelled to genuflect to, and tremble before, the supremacy of this ultimate threat, upon pain of being cast aside as some sort of anti-American, terrorist-loving radical.

That we are a strong enough nation to defeat terrorism without fundamentally changing our nation is a message that Americans are clearly ready to hear. We are more than four years away from September 11, 2001, and despite the dire warnings of the Bush administration, people in rural Kansas and suburban Georgia and everywhere else are beginning to realize that on the list of problems and threats that endanger their children and impede their dreams, the potential of a terrorist attack does not predominate.

In a rational world, risk is equal to impact multiplied by probability. As the Linguasphere Dictionary puts it: "In professional risk assessment, risk combines the probability of a negative event occurring with how harmful that event would be." But the administration has spent four years urging Americans to ignore that way of thinking and instead assent to any government measure, no matter the costs of comparative harms, as long as it is pursued in the name of fighting this ultimate evil.

But one can protect against the threat of terrorism with courage, calm, and resolve—the attributes that have always defined our nation as it has confronted other threats, including many at least as significant. Hysteria and fear-mongering are the opposite of strength. The strong remain rational and unafraid.

Most people know individuals in their lives who live in this type of irrational, all-consuming fear—people who are scared, pathologically risk-averse, always hiding and exerting excess caution lest something go wrong. In its more extreme version, that sort of fear manifests as a life-destroying mental disorder. It is a pitiful image, and such people typically achieve very little. They cannot, because their fear is paralyzing.

The Bush administration has been trying for four years to reduce this country to a collective version of that affliction. And it is hard to imagine what a nation fueled by such fear can accomplish.

The administration has managed to get away with the Orwellian idea that fear is the hallmark of courage, and a rational and calm approach is a mark of cowardice. They have been aided in this effort by a frightened national media and political elite that lives in Washington and New York—two "target-rich" cities—and that has been so petrified of further attacks that they were easily pushed into a state of passive, uncritical compliance in exchange for promises of protection. But we now have some emotional distance from the shock of September 11, and the power of that fear weapon is diminishing.

We must now see that fear is a by-product of weakness and cowardice. A strong nation does not give up its freedoms or sacrifice its national character in the face of manufactured fear and panic. But that is what George Bush has spent the last four years urging the country to do, and it is what he is counting on—that this NSA lawbreaking scandal will soon join the litany of other scandals that have inconsequentially receded in the public consciousness.

Freedom Fighters

For a different vision of our nation, we need only look to the founders, who embodied courage and resolve. Most of them were wealthy and educated and enjoyed the privileges of a gentrified upbringing in the British Empire. Almost to a person, their wealth and status enabled them to lead comfortable, usually luxurious lives, with ample material comforts, opportunities, and unthreatened safety.

But mere comfort and safety were not enough for them. What they lacked were the basic liberties that have now come to define America and that we now take for granted. They demanded that those liberties be granted to them; when they were refused by the British king, they waged a war against the most powerful armed force on earth. They risked everything—luxury and privilege, material wealth, and life itself—not because they were forced to, or because that war was imposed on them. They *chose* that war. They chose to risk everything, because they valued liberty and freedom over everything else. That is why the words of Patrick Henry— "Give me liberty or give me death"—have had such resonance with Americans ever since he uttered them in 1775. That willingness to fight against tyranny, and sacrifice safety and comforts for liberty and freedom, is the essence of the American character. These are the values that define strength, courage, and resolve in our country, and they always have.

Under the Bush administration, we have traveled as a nation from the towering heights defined by the courage and impassioned stance of Patrick Henry and other American founders to a fearful and craven basement where we are ready to give up our liberties and grant the government power without limits because we are afraid.

Senator John Cornyn is a Texas Republican and, as such, one of the most loyal defenders of George Bush. On December 20, 2005—five days after *The New York Times* first revealed the president's lawless eavesdropping—the Capitol Hill newspaper *The Hill* reported on the debates that had arisen in Congress over these issues:

> Senators launched new salvos in the battle over national security and civil liberties yesterday as recent revelations of domestic spying continued to color the chamber's stalemate on an extension of the antiterrorism law known as the PATRIOT Act.
>
> "None of your civil liberties matter much after you're dead," said Sen. John Cornyn (R-Texas), a former judge and close ally of the president who sits on the Judiciary Committee.

Another of President Bush's most loyal defenders, Senator Pat Roberts of Kansas, mouthed almost the same precise words on February 3, 2006, at a hearing of the Senate Intelligence Committee, which he chairs: "I would only point out that you really don't have any civil liberties if you're dead." Like Cornyn, Roberts made this comment in the course of defending the president's illegal eavesdropping on Americans.

Contrast the American ethos as embodied by Patrick Henry and the other founders—an insistence that our system of government adhere to the rule of law and preserve individual liberty—with the fear-driven mentality peddled by the president's defenders in order to justify his conduct. We are told that we must give up our liberties and allow the president the power to break the law, because none of that really matters. What matters is that you let the government protect you.

Where would America be if, throughout our history, we had succumbed to the paralyzed, weak-willed fear being hawked by the likes of Cornyn and Roberts? We would not have risked our lives to win our freedom from the British monarchy. We would have acquiesced to the evils of slavery and the division of our country rather than risk our lives in the Civil War. After Pearl Harbor, we would have gone to war against Japan but not Nazi Germany; after all, Germany had not attacked us, and if our *own* freedoms are not worth risking our lives for, why on earth would we risk them to protect strangers from Nazi tyranny? We would have found a way to get along with the Soviet Union, even if it meant acquiescing while they set up dictatorships around the globe; after all, they had nuclear missiles aimed at our country, and the freedom of distant peoples would have mattered less to us than our own security. But that is not the America that has become the freest and most powerful nation on earth.

Once we choose to assuage our fears rather than protect our liberties, the type of fear being promoted by the administration and its supporters compels us to relinquish our freedoms, endorse government excesses, and sacrifice everything that distinguishes America and has made it great and worth fighting for. Attempting to persuade Americans to adopt this fear-driven mentality has become the first priority of the administration.

On January 28, 2006, history professor and best-selling author Joseph J. Ellis published an op-ed in *The New York Times* in which he pointed out one of the most important and under-recognized truths about the way in which we view the threat of terrorism:

> My first question: where does Sept. 11 rank in the grand sweep of American history as a threat to national security? By my calculations it does not make the top tier of the list, which requires the threat to pose a serious challenge to the survival of the American republic.
>
> Here is my version of the top tier: the War for Independence, where defeat meant no United States of America; the War of 1812, when the national capital was burned to the ground; the Civil War,

which threatened the survival of the Union; World War II, which represented a totalitarian threat to democracy and capitalism; the cold war, most specifically the Cuban missile crisis of 1962, which made nuclear annihilation a distinct possibility.

Sept. 11 does not rise to that level of threat because, while it places lives and lifestyles at risk, it does not threaten the survival of the American republic, *even though the terrorists would like us to believe so.* [Emphasis added.]

And the terrorists appear to be joined in that desire by President Bush. His administration continuously—and irrationally—depicts terrorism as the overarching threat around which we are constructing our entire foreign policy, changing the basic principles of our government, and fundamentally altering both our behavior in the world and the way we are perceived.

As a result, one rarely hears anyone arguing that the terrorism threat, like any other threat, should be viewed in perspective and subjected to rational risk-benefit assessments. That is because opinions about terrorism are the new form of political correctness, and even hinting that this threat is not the all-consuming, existential danger to our republic portrayed by the White House is liable to draw questions about one's patriotism and one's sanity.

In his op-ed, Professor Ellis makes another critically important point: Even with regard to the genuinely existential threats in our nation's history, we have at times allowed our fears to be exploited. But when we have done so, we have adopted excessive measures which have led to some of the most shameful episodes in our past. Among the examples he cites are the Alien and Sedition Acts in 1798, "which allowed the federal government to close newspapers and deport foreigners during the 'quasi-war' with France," and the internment of Japanese Americans during World War II, "which was justified on the grounds that their ancestry made them potential threats to national security."

The cause of our irrationality today, our inability to view the terrorism threat with any historical perspective, is not a mystery. Terrorist groups like Al Qaeda deliberately stage attacks designed to instill fear in the population far beyond what is warranted by their actual threat level. And our government has been working towards the same goal—attempting to convince us that all of our nation's principles must be sacrificed in the name of guarding against this threat.

But there are all sorts of serious threats which America faces, including the threat of overreacting to threats. As Professor Ellis concludes: "History suggests that we have faced greater challenges and triumphed, and that overreaction is a greater danger than complacency."

Life During Wartime

Supporters of the president often defend his lawless expansion of executive power by equating it to Abraham Lincoln's suspension of habeas corpus and other emergency measures taken to save the Union during the Civil War. Bush supporter Frank Gaffney, in a December 19, 2005, column on Townhall.com, offered an illustrative version of this claim:

> In the Civil War, Abraham Lincoln infuriated civil libertarians by suspending for the duration the touchstone right of habeas corpus. It appears that in this War for the Free World, we are about to suspend common sense—at least until the next, possibly catastrophic attack demonstrates anew what the latest terrorist murder in Iraq showed all-too-graphically: We will enjoy no civil liberties if we are destroyed.

Invoking the nation-threatening crises faced by Abraham Lincoln to justify George Bush's current lawbreaking is breathtaking in both its dishonesty and rank fear-mongering.

During Lincoln's presidency, the entire nation was engulfed in an internal, all-out war. Half of the country was fully devoted to the destruction of the other half. The existence of the nation was very much in doubt. Americans were dying violent deaths every day at a staggering rate. One million Americans were wounded and a half million others—a full 5 percent of the population—died, making it the deadliest war America has ever faced. On multiple occasions, more than 25,000 Americans, and sometimes as many as 50,000, were killed in battles lasting no more than three days. The scope of carnage, killing, and chaos—all within the country, on American soil—is difficult to comprehend.

And if one insists that it is appropriate to call our conflict against groups like Al Qaeda a war, this "war" could not be more unlike the Civil War, both in the amount of death and destruction it causes and how it affects the daily lives of Americans. The word *war* has become an all-purpose political tool, to the point where it is virtually impoverished of meaning. War is something we wage on cancer, on poverty, on drugs, and now on "terror." Wars now come in the cold variety; the traditional form against other countries, as in Iraq; and vague, interminable conflicts with ill-defined enemies who are capable of limited strikes once every few years.

But whatever else one can say about our conflict with terrorists—even if one insists on calling it a war—it is nothing even remotely like the Civil War, when the existence of the nation was in doubt and the whole country was engulfed by killing and anarchy. That defenders of President Bush now invoke the incomparably severe crisis of the Civil War—and hail the dangerous revocations of liberty which that crisis necessitated—gives a clear idea as to how extreme their fear-driven perspective is, and how radical their "pro-security" aspirations have become.

More Safe, Less Free

In March 2006, researchers in the social psychology program at Rutgers University–New Brunswick offered some empirical evidence to demonstrate the critical role fear plays in driving people to support George Bush. Their study sought to measure the impact fear had on voting choices in the 2004 election. As the summary issued by Rutgers recounted:

> Their findings demonstrated that registered voters in a psychologically benign state of mind preferred Senator Kerry to President Bush, but Bush was more popular than Kerry after voters received a subtle reminder of death. Citing an Osama bin Laden tape that surfaced a few days before the election, among other factors, the authors state, "the present study adds convergent support to the idea that George W. Bush's victory in the 2004 presidential election was facilitated by Americans' nonconscious concerns about death. . . ." The authors believe that people were scared into voting for Bush.

More than 130 registered voters participated in the study. Split into two groups, the first group was asked to write down a description of their emotions regarding the thought of their own death and, as specifically as possible, write down what will physically happen when they die and after they are dead. The second group responded to parallel questions regarding watching television. Within the first group 32 responded that they would vote for Bush and 14 opted for Kerry. In the second group, the decision was reversed as 34 selected Kerry and 8 selected Bush.

The Bush administration did not, of course, invent the use of fear as a weapon to justify its wrongful conduct and enhance its own power. That tactic was well known to the founders of our country, who warned us of it repeatedly, and is a danger that has been recognized, and condemned, by our nation's greatest leaders.

Nor, of course, is Al Qaeda the first enemy the United States has had. The Soviet Union had hundreds of nuclear missiles pointed at every large American city for years. And while the nation succumbed to the excesses of McCarthyism—which were enabled by fear-mongering over a genuine threat—America had strong and brave leaders who refused to allow the country to relinquish its values and principles in the name of fighting this external threat.

On April 24, 1950, President Harry S Truman gave a speech to the nation regarding the threat posed by domestic communism—a threat at least as real as Islamic terrorism. This is part of what he said:

> Now I am going to tell you how we are not going to fight communism. We are not going to transform our fine FBI into a Gestapo secret police. That is what some people would like to do. We are not going to try to control what our people read and say and think. We are not going to turn the United States into a right-wing totalitarian country in order to deal with a left-wing totalitarian threat.

And the founders repeatedly warned of the danger, and the likelihood, that governments would attempt to exploit fear of external threats in order to justify abridgments of core liberties. As Hamilton explained in Federalist No. 8:

Safety from external danger is the most powerful director of national conduct. Even the ardent love of liberty will, after a time, give way to its dictates. The violent destruction of life and property incident to war; the continual effort and alarm attendant on a state of continual danger, will compel nations the most attached to liberty, to resort for repose and security to institutions which have a tendency to destroy their civil and political rights. To be more safe, they, at length, become willing to run the risk of being less free.

Fear has never been a defining attribute of the American character, in part because the founders of the country were so aware of its corrosive and toxic effect on liberty. In *Thoughts on Government*, John Adams wrote:

Fear is the foundation of most governments; but it is so sordid and brutal a passion, and renders men in whose breasts it predominates so stupid and miserable, that Americans will not be likely to approve of any political institution which is founded on it.

With great prescience, these warnings describe exactly that tactic which the Bush administration and its supporters use in insisting that Americans give up their basic liberties in exchange for promises of "protection" from these dangers.

The apex of this fear-wallowing came during the exceptionally well-staged Republican National Convention of 2004, where one Republican speaker after the next shrieked that we must reelect George Bush because only he could make us safe, only he could protect us from the terrorists. Here is Zell Miller, the former Democratic senator from Georgia, explaining how his fears drove him to support George Bush:

And like you, I ask which leader is it today that has the vision, the willpower, and, yes, the backbone to best protect my family?

The clear answer to that question has placed me in this hall with you tonight. For my family is more important than my Party.

There is but one man to whom I am willing to entrust their future and that man's name is George W. Bush. . . .

I have knocked on the door of this man's soul and found someone home, a God-fearing man with a good heart and a spine of tempered steel—the man I trust to protect my most precious possession: my family.

In this view, George Bush is not just an elected official, but the protector of our families. The president himself almost invariably invokes this formula, which the founders warned against—that Americans ought to permit government abuses and abridgments of liberty in order to be protected against the threat of terrorism—whenever he seeks to justify or defend his conduct. In one speech he gave on January 23, 2006, devoted to a discussion of terrorism issues and a defense of his illegal eavesdropping, he insisted on four separate occasions that we need not worry ourselves about any concerns over what the government is doing because it is all being done to "protect" us:

> I resolved on that day to do everything I can to protect the American people. . . .
>   My most important job is to protect the security of the American people. . . .
>   And so part of my decision-making process, part of it as you see when I begin to protect you, to do my number one priority, rests upon this fact . . .
>   If they're making phone calls into the United States, we need to know why—to protect you.

Invoking the threat of terrorism and the president's proclaimed commitment to "protect" us from those threats is the administration's sole and all-purpose defense of its conduct.

The administration also makes relentless use of a closely related tactic—to accuse critics of the administration of actually wanting to help the terrorists attack America. As but one illustrative example, here is what Karl Rove, the president's top advisor, said in a January 20, 2006, speech regarding the NSA lawbreaking scandal, as reported by *The New York Times*'s Adam Nagourney: "Let me be as clear as I can be: President Bush believes if Al Qaeda is calling somebody in America, it is in our national security interest to know who they're calling and why," Mr. Rove said. "Some important Democrats clearly disagree."

This statement, of course, is factually false, and Rove knows that.

Nobody of any note—let alone "some important Democrats"—believes that it's not "in our national security interest to know" whom Al Qaeda is calling and why. Nobody opposes eavesdropping on Al Qaeda, and Rove knows that. And yet, here he is, claiming that the NSA scandal is based on a disagreement about whether the government should be eavesdropping on Al Qaeda.

The statement is designed, as always, to exploit fears of terrorism by insinuating that anyone who opposes the administration or objects to their seizure of ever-expanding illegal powers is endangering the lives of Americans and is actually on the side of the terrorists. The tacit assumption is that one can only oppose terrorism by endorsing whatever the administration wants. The administration knows only one tactic—the attempt to place Americans in as much fear as possible, fear that unless the Bush administration is free to operate without restraints and without opposition, their lives are endangered. It is a tactic as manipulative as it is transparent, and yet it has been wielded by the administration as its response to every accusation, every scandal, and every controversy.

We do not have a government where the president can break the law in secret and then tell us not to worry about it because it is being done to "protect" us. We have never had a system of government operate on such paternalistic and blindly loyal sentiments. And we have never before been a nation living in such fear that, in exchange for promises of protection and safety, we are told that we must allow the president to seize those very powers which the Constitution prohibits.

The president's embrace of radical theories of presidential power threatens to change the system of government we have. But worse still, his administration's relentless, never-ending attempts to keep the nation in a state of fear can also change the kind of nation we are. Hysteria and paranoia have never been part of the American national character, but along with the founding principles of our republic, the Bush administration has been attempting to change that, too.

CHAPTER SIX

Fate of the Union

The Watergate Lesson

Ever since the president's secret, warrantless eavesdropping program was revealed in December 2005, his supporters have repeatedly and loudly boasted that this scandal would not harm his presidency. And when, after several weeks, the sky had not fallen in on the White House, the president's aides paraded around, full of hubris, trumpeting that the scandal had blown over without consequence and insisting that Americans did not object to the president's violations of the law.

Working in tandem with them in disseminating that message were the national media, which have a short attention span and have rarely conveyed to the country the actual theories of power underlying the administration's lawbreaking. Nor have the media generated much debate about, or explanation of, the ramifications for our country if we simply allow the administration to break the law and to seize these radical powers with impunity.

The government actions we have been witnessing since 2001—lawless detentions of American citizens, illegal use of torture, a president who openly and defiantly claims he is above the law—are too extreme and extraordinary to forever evade meaningful scrutiny and a real debate by Americans.

Anyone who believes that the president will not be held accountable for the NSA scandal and these other incidents of lawbreaking has not learned one of the key lessons of the Watergate scandal, which forced President Richard M. Nixon from office in 1974.

As Watergate showed so clearly, a real debate over a president's radical—and illegal—actions is inevitable. It takes time for abuses of power by government officials to come to light and for the full extent of their dangers to be understood and appreciated. Scandals of this sort do not resolve themselves overnight. But once Americans focus on the government's conduct and come to recognize its dangerous and intolerable nature, there is no question that they will render the final judgment on what will be tolerated from our political leaders and what will be resoundingly rejected.

On June 17, 1972, five burglars with connections to the CIA and other Republican power centers were caught breaking into the Democratic National Committee headquarters at the Watergate Hotel in Washington, D.C. The burglars had come to adjust bugging equipment they had previously installed and to photograph documents. For months after the burglary, it was conventional wisdom in both political parties and among the national media that the scandal had no chance of inflicting any political harm on President Nixon—who, in stark contrast to President Bush now, was highly popular when the scandal began. A full six months after the burglary, in November 1972, President Nixon was reelected in one of the most lopsided presidential elections in our nation's history, winning every state but Massachusetts. Certainly by that point it was assumed that the Watergate scandal would be relegated to a historical footnote, an irrelevant sideshow involving some minor abuses, which Americans were prepared to accept.

In early 1973, as the scandal began to engulf more and more of Nixon's close aides, the public had still not concluded that the crimes were sufficiently serious to warrant abandoning, let alone impeaching, the president. In the February 7, 1998, *Congressional Quarterly*, Ronald D. Elving recounts the history:

> While the revelations accumulated, the rest of the country tuned out. That November, Nixon carried 49 states in winning re-election. More than two months later, as the first Watergate defendants were going to court in January 1973, Nixon's numbers in the Gallup Poll were among the most robust of his presidency: 68 percent approval to 25 percent disapproval. . . .

Only when the president began to resist investigations into the burglary and its cover-up did the public begin to wonder what he had to hide. But while the president's stonewalling finally caused Americans to become more interested in the scandal, they still refused to conclude that he had engaged in serious wrongdoing, even as many of his closest aides resigned. Elving continues:

Of course, that was before Nixon began talking about invoking executive privilege to prevent White House aides from testifying about an alleged cover-up. When that key phrase, "executive privilege," became part of the discussion, Nixon's numbers started their descent.

In February, the Senate voted 70-0 to empanel an investigating committee of its own. Nixon's approval rating in the first week of April stood at 54 percent in the Gallup Poll. Most Americans were still withholding judgment. Even after the April 30 speech in which Nixon announced the resignation of his closest aides, many Republicans continued to rally around the president.

Because Americans—almost a full year after the Watergate scandal was first revealed—still had not concluded that the president had acted wrongfully, Republican leaders, and even some prominent Democrats, were willing to rally around the president and insist that, for the good of the country, he not be punished for the crimes that had been committed. As Elving recounts, Republican leaders like Senator Hugh C. Scott of Pennsylvania and California Governor Ronald Reagan defended Nixon; Reagan said that the Watergate burglars were "not criminals at heart." Vice President Spiro T. Agnew accused the press of "McCarthyism." Even some Democrats were still defending the president at that point, with Senator William Proxmire complaining that the media had been "grossly unfair" to Nixon.

But throughout this time, investigative journalists, led by Bob Woodward and Carl Bernstein at *The Washington Post*, were uncovering the incriminating evidence the administration was attempting to conceal. Journalists at the nation's leading newspapers obtained reams of classified information from sources inside the government, who were determined not to allow the Nixon administration to break the law with impunity and then cover up their crimes.

Investigating alongside the journalists was Congress. Committees began using their subpoena power to obtain documents and question witnesses in order to determine who was responsible for the break-in and the subsequent cover-up. As a result of these journalistic and congressional inquiries, it became impossible for Americans to ignore the president's misconduct any longer. As Elving recounts,

By then, however [when the president's party leaders were rallying around him], the bleeding in the Gallup Poll had dropped Nixon to just 48 percent approval in the first week of May—a drop of 20 percentage points since January. And that rating would keep on falling through the 25 percent level before Nixon's resignation in August 1974.

During the Watergate scandal, the Nixon administration engaged in all sorts of subterfuge to derail the investigations. The notorious Saturday Night Massacre occurred when the president ordered his attorney general, Elliot Richardson, to fire Archibald Cox, the special prosecutor investigating the scandal. Richardson refused, as did his deputy, so Nixon fired them and turned to the next man in line at the Justice Department, Robert Bork, who was willing to fire Cox.

Such obstructionist efforts fueled the scandal even more and emboldened Nixon's opponents to pursue other ways of ensuring that he and his administration were held accountable for their lawbreaking. Public opinion was so inflamed by the Saturday Night Massacre that it was shortly thereafter that articles of impeachment were introduced in Congress for the first time.

Americans do not lightly conclude that their president has committed crimes or engaged in wrongdoing. Respect for the office ensures that Americans will reach this conclusion only when they are certain that the evidence compellingly demonstrates abuses of power that will hurt the nation and are therefore intolerable.

President Nixon failed in his efforts to conceal his wrongdoing from the public. His cover-up was illuminated by investigative journalists, who aggressively pursued incriminating evidence that the administration had attempted to conceal by classifying it and forbidding its dissemination. And Congress fulfilled its oversight responsibilities, holding hearings and investigating to determine whether the administration's claims were truthful.

But most of all, President Nixon was held accountable for his wrongdoing and abuses of power because Americans, with the relevant evidence assembled by the press and by Congress, concluded that he had seized powers that were not rightfully his to exercise. As a result, they demanded that he be forced from office, because preserving the American system of government from those who sought to assault and violate it took precedence over partisan allegiances.

It took a full year after the break-in—during which top Nixon aides resigned and there were highly publicized attempts by the administration to block investigations—before Americans began, gradually and reluctantly, to conclude that the president had committed serious wrongdoing. And it took another year for Americans to demand that the president be held accountable and that he be forced from office. Eventually, with impeachment a foregone conclusion, President Richard Nixon went on national television on August 8, 1974, to announce that he would resign the next day.

That two-year process—from burglary to resignation—was enabled by the checks and balances the founders instituted in order to safeguard our system of government: namely, a free and aggressive press, a Congress that takes its oversight duties seriously, and the reservation of ultimate power in the hands of the American people.

Nothing to Hide?

While Americans were able to discover the truth about Watergate as a result of congressional investigations and aggressive journalism, in the warrantless eavesdropping scandal the Bush administration has engaged in a concerted scheme to block and intimidate both those institutions. It has thus far succeeded in concealing from the American people numerous facts that would shed light on its conduct.

Ever since the NSA eavesdropping scandal began to emerge, in December 2005, the White House has emphatically maintained that it has done nothing wrong and therefore has nothing to hide. Nevertheless, many congressional officials—including many Republicans—announced that the oversight duties of Congress compelled them to investigate this controversy and to report to the American public on basic questions, such as what the secret program involved, how extensive it was, and why it was kept from Congress and the FISA courts.

Back in 2001, the Bush administration prevented the judiciary— specifically, the FISA court—from exercising the oversight function assigned to it by Congress, and simply ignored the requirement that warrants must be obtained from the court before any eavesdropping could take place. And since *The New York Times* disclosed the president's decision to eavesdrop in violation of the law, the administration—contrary to its assurances that it had nothing to hide—has aggressively blocked all efforts by Congress to even find out what happened, using as its primary obstructive weapon the fact that both houses of Congress are controlled by the president's own party.

What happened when the Senate Intelligence Committee showed an interest in investigating the nature and scope of this secret eavesdropping program is particularly revealing. This committee was an outgrowth of the post-Watergate Church Committee of 1975, which investigated the intelligence abuses perpetrated over decades by the government. The current Intelligence Committee's official oversight function is stated as follows:

> To oversee and make continuing studies of the intelligence activities and programs of the United States Government, and to submit to the Senate appropriate proposals for legislation and report to the Senate concerning such intelligence activities and programs. In carrying out this purpose, the Select Committee on Intelligence shall make every effort to assure that the appropriate departments and agencies of the United States provide informed and timely intelligence necessary for the executive and legislative branches to make sound decisions affecting the security and vital interests of the Nation. It is further the purpose of this resolution *to provide vigilant legislative oversight over the intelligence activities of the United States to assure that such activities are in conformity with the Constitution and laws of the United States.*" [Emphasis added.]

Investigating a controversial eavesdropping program aimed at Americans is precisely the kind of purpose envisioned for this committee. Even several Republicans on the committee, including Olympia Snowe of Maine and Chuck Hagel of Nebraska, emphatically and publicly stated that a joint investigation by the Senate Intelligence and Judiciary committees into the president's secret eavesdropping was urgently needed. "Revelations that the U.S. government has conducted domestic electronic surveillance without express legal authority indeed warrants congressional examination," Snowe said in a statement issued on December 21, 2005. "I believe the Congress—as a coequal branch of government—must immediately and expeditiously review the use of this practice."

On the same date, Senators Snowe and Hagel signed a letter addressed to the leaders of the Judiciary and Intelligence committees, which said in part:

> We write to express our profound concern about recent revelations that the United States Government may have engaged in domestic electronic surveillance without appropriate legal authority. These allegations, which the President, at least in part, confirmed this weekend, require immediate inquiry and action by the Senate.
>
> We respectfully request that the Select Committee on Intelligence and the Committee on the Judiciary, which share jurisdiction and oversight of this issue, jointly undertake an inquiry into the facts and law surrounding these allegations. The overlapping jurisdiction of these two Committees is particularly critical where civil liberties and the rule of law hang in the balance. . . .
>
> It is critical that Congress determine, as quickly as possible, exactly what collection activities were authorized, what were actually undertaken, how many names and numbers were involved over what period, and what was the asserted legal authority for such activities. In sum, we must determine the facts. . . .
>
> We have extensively debated these issues. At no time, to our knowledge, did any administration representative ask the Congress to consider amending existing law to permit electronic surveillance of suspected terrorists without a warrant such as outlined in the *New York Times* article.
>
> We strongly believe that the Judiciary and Intelligence Committees should immediately seek to answer the factual and legal questions which surround these revelations, and recommend appropriate action to the Senate.

Senator Jay Rockefeller of West Virginia, the ranking minority member on the Intelligence Committee, introduced a motion in early February 2006 to have the committee investigate the scope and extent of the president's warrantless eavesdropping program. Among the questions Rockefeller believed the committee must seek answers to were: How many Americans did the secret NSA program target? On what basis were those Americans selected for surveillance? How many innocent Americans, with no connection to Al Qaeda or any terrorist group, were targeted? Did the administration eavesdrop on domestic communications of Americans? Did the administration initiate any other warrantless eavesdropping programs aimed at Americans? Why did the administration never seek revisions to FISA if it believed that the law was inadequate or too cumbersome to permit necessary eavesdropping?

Eight votes were needed to approve Senator Rockefeller's motion. The Senate Intelligence Committee has eight Republicans and seven Democrats, but because two Republicans—Snowe and Hagel—had already insisted upon an investigation, and a third, Senator Mike DeWine of Ohio, had also indicated support, it appeared certain that the Senate would finally obtain some answers.

That is when the White House made its move to quash the investigation. It worked feverishly behind the scenes to pressure every Republican to vote against Senator Rockefeller's motion. The vote was originally scheduled by the committee chairman, Republican Senator Pat Roberts of Kansas, for February 16, 2006. The day before, on February 15, *The Washington Post* published an article detailing the frenzied and relentless pressure being personally exerted on committee Republicans by Vice President Dick Cheney to kill the proposed investigation:

> Congress appeared ready to launch an investigation into the Bush administration's warrantless domestic surveillance program last week, but an all-out White House lobbying campaign has dramatically slowed the effort and may kill it, key Republican and Democratic sources said yesterday.
>
> The Senate intelligence committee is scheduled to vote tomorrow on a Democratic-sponsored motion to start an inquiry into the recently revealed program in which the National Security Agency eavesdrops on an undisclosed number of phone calls and e-mails involving U.S. residents without obtaining warrants from a secret court. Two committee Democrats said the panel—made up of eight Republicans and seven Democrats—was clearly leaning in favor of the motion last week but now is closely divided and possibly inclined against it.
>
> They attributed the shift to last week's closed briefings given by top administration officials to the full House and Senate intelligence

committees, and to private appeals to wavering GOP senators by officials, including Vice President Cheney. "It's been a full-court press," said a top Senate Republican aide who asked to speak only on background—as did several others for this story—because of the classified nature of the intelligence committees' work.

Despite Cheney's arm-twisting, on the day of the scheduled vote, February 16, it appeared that Senator Rockefeller's motion might yet be approved. But Senator Roberts prevented a vote that day by adjourning the committee meeting before the vote could be held. After that procedural maneuver, Senator Roberts promised that the vote would be held on March 7, 2006.

Newsweek reported on February 20, 2006, that the three Republican senators—Snowe, Hagel, and DeWine—were "expected to join with the Democrats on the committee to vote to demand more information about the secret eavesdropping program from the White House and intelligence agencies."

Apparently, the White House lobbying was relentless—and effective. On March 7, the Committee met and finally voted. The motion to investigate was rejected on an 8 to 7 party-line vote—with each and every one of the eight Republicans voting not even to conduct an investigation into the Republican president's conduct in eavesdropping on Americans in violation of the law.

Thus, the same White House that insisted from the beginning of this scandal that it had nothing to hide and would welcome a full investigation secretly pressured Senate Republicans to ensure that no investigation occurred. As a result, this highly controversial and plainly illegal eavesdropping program has thus far gone uninvestigated, even by the very committee with a mandate to exercise oversight over the president's surveillance activities.

The administration's efforts to block investigations into its conduct have become so severe that even its most reliable congressional allies are publicly accusing the administration of stonewalling. As FOXNews.com reported regarding an April 5, 2006, hearing of the House Judiciary Committee into the NSA program:

The Republican chairman of the House Judiciary Committee point-edly criticized Attorney General Alberto Gonzales Thursday for "stonewalling" by refusing to answer questions about the Bush administration's warrantless eavesdropping program.

Rep. James Sensenbrenner, R-Wis., said Gonzales was frustrat-ing his panel's oversight of the Justice Department and the contro-versial surveillance by declining to provide information about how the program is reviewed inside the administration and by whom.

"How can we discharge our oversight if, every time we ask a pointed question, we're told the program is classified?" Sensenbren-ner asked Gonzales near the start of a lengthy hearing on the depart-ment's activities. "I think that . . . is stonewalling."

That the president's most stalwart Republican allies are publicly con-demning the administration for covering up their behavior is a potent reflection of how extreme its conduct has become.

As a result of the administration's stonewalling, we still know virtu-ally no details about the secret NSA program—which Americans were eavesdropped on, how and why they were selected, whether innocent Americans with no connection to terrorism were eavesdropped on, what was done with the information, and how many Americans were subject to this secret surveillance.

Muzzling the Media

When the courts and Congress are either unable or unwilling to provide checks, balances, and oversight on presidential abuses of power, it remains up to the press to perform this function—as it did so well dur-ing the Watergate scandal. But the Bush administration's efforts to pre-vent the press from investigating and reporting on its illegal eavesdropping activities have been as successful—if not more so—than its efforts to prevent oversight from the judicial and congressional branches of government.

Three days after the *Times* disclosed the existence of the illegal eaves-dropping program, on December 19, 2005, *Newsweek*'s Jonathan Alter reported that the president had summoned the editor and publisher of

The New York Times to the Oval Office in early December to persuade the newspaper to essentially kill the story. As Alter explained:

> No wonder Bush was so desperate that *The New York Times* not publish its story on the National Security Agency eavesdropping on American citizens without a warrant, in what lawyers outside the administration say is a clear violation of the 1978 Foreign Intelligence Surveillance Act. I learned this week that on Dec. 6, Bush summoned Times publisher Arthur Sulzberger and executive editor Bill Keller to the Oval Office in a futile attempt to talk them out of running the story. The *Times* will not comment on the meeting, but one can only imagine the president's desperation.
>
> The problem was not that the disclosures would compromise national security, as Bush claimed at his press conference. His comparison to the damaging pre-9/11 revelation of Osama bin Laden's use of a satellite phone, which caused bin Laden to change tactics, is fallacious; any Americans with ties to Muslim extremists—in fact, all American Muslims, period—have long since suspected that the U.S. government might be listening in to their conversations. Bush claimed that "the fact that we are discussing this program is helping the enemy." But there is simply no evidence, or even reasonable presumption, that this is so. And rather than the leaking being a "shameful act," it was the work of a patriot inside the government who was trying to stop a presidential power grab.
>
> No, Bush was desperate to keep the *Times* from running this important story—which the paper had already inexplicably held for a year—because he knew that it would reveal him as a law-breaker. He insists he had "legal authority derived from the Constitution and congressional resolution authorizing force." But the Constitution explicitly requires the president to obey the law. And the post 9/11 congressional resolution authorizing "all necessary force" in fighting terrorism was made in clear reference to military intervention. It did not scrap the Constitution and allow the president to do whatever he pleased in any area in the name of fighting terrorism.

It is not, of course, uncommon for newspapers to learn about government secrets but refrain from publishing those secrets, if their disclosure would (a) serve no journalistic purpose and promote no public good, and (b) endanger national security. Almost every newspaper, for instance, would refrain from publishing information about imminent troop movements in a time of war, because there is no value in publishing it and its disclosure would endanger American soldiers.

But neither of those justifications applied here, even arguably. The story served a compelling public interest: we learned that our government was breaking the law when eavesdropping on us. And it posed no conceivable security threat. The story published no technical details about the program, and so it only told our enemies what they already knew—that the Bush administration was eavesdropping on their conversations. Of course the administration was, and of course the terrorists knew it. The president himself said publicly many times that they were doing so. The significance of the story the *Times* withheld for more than a full year was not the that administration was eavesdropping, but that it was eavesdropping *in violation of the law*.

Once the *Times* finally rediscovered its journalistic purpose and published the story, on December 15, its editor apparently realized that the newspaper had never had any excuse for waiting a year to do so. In response to inquiries from *Salon*'s Tim Grieve as to why it finally published this story, the *Times* issued a statement from Executive Editor Bill Keller:

> In the course of subsequent reporting we satisfied ourselves that we could write about this program—withholding a number of technical details—in a way that would not expose any intelligence-gathering methods or capabilities that are not already on the public record. The fact that the government eavesdrops on those suspected of terrorist connections is well known.
>
> The fact that the NSA can legally monitor communications within the United States with a warrant from the Foreign Intelligence Surveillance Court is also public information. What is new is that the NSA has for the past three years had the authority to eavesdrop on Americans and others inside the United States without a warrant. It is that expansion of authority—not the need for a robust anti-terror intelligence operation—that prompted debate within the government, and that is the subject of the article.

That defense amounts to a serious understatement. Disclosing that the surveillance program was being conducted illegally never constituted a national security threat. The only "threat" arising from disclosure of this information would be to the political and legal interests of the Bush administration, not to the security interests of the United States.

The president and his aides have attacked and threatened those responsible for exposure of their lawless behavior, and the media are quite aware of these threats. In the president's very first press conference following the disclosure of the illegal eavesdropping, on December 19, 2005, he essentially accused whoever spoke out about this surveillance of committing treason. The president warned:

> There is a process that goes on inside the Justice Department about leaks, and I presume that process is moving forward. My personal opinion is it was a shameful act for someone to disclose this very important program in a time of war. The fact that we're discussing this program is helping the enemy. . . .
>
> You've got to understand—and I hope the American people understand—there is still an enemy that would like to strike the United States of America, and they're very dangerous. And the discussion about how we try to find them will enable them to adjust. . . .
> But it is a shameful act by somebody who has got secrets of the United States government and feels like they need to disclose them publicly.

As a result of these presidential threats, one could almost sense the fear of the defensive *Times* reporters as they described the White House threats the following day:

> Mr. Bush strongly hinted that the government was beginning a leak investigation into how the existence of the program was disclosed. It was first revealed in an article published on *The New York Times* Web site on Thursday night, though some information that administration officials argued could be useful to terrorists had been omitted.

As the White House continued throughout January and February 2006 to block congressional investigations into its secret eavesdropping activities, the media continued to attempt to discover the truth about what the administration did. As a result, administration attacks on—and threats against—the investigative journalists covering this story have been intensifying significantly.

For example, on February 12, 2006, *The New York Times* reported that the president's political appointees at the Justice Department are considering criminal prosecution of those who brought the administration's illegal conduct to light, including James Risen and other investigative journalists at the *Times*. According to the *Times* article:

> Federal agents have interviewed officials at several of the country's law enforcement and national security agencies in a rapidly expanding criminal investigation into the circumstances surrounding a New York Times article published in December that disclosed the existence of a highly classified domestic eavesdropping program, according to government officials.
>
> The investigation, which appears to cover the case from 2004, when the newspaper began reporting the story, is being closely coordinated with criminal prosecutors at the Justice Department, the officials said. People who have been interviewed and others in the government who have been briefed on the interviews said the investigation seemed to lay the groundwork for a grand jury inquiry that could lead to criminal charges. . . .
>
> At the same time, conservatives have attacked the disclosure of classified information as an illegal act, demanding a vigorous investigative effort to find and prosecute whoever disclosed classified information.
>
> An upcoming article in Commentary magazine suggests that the newspaper might be prosecuted for violations of the Espionage Act and said, "What The New York Times has done is nothing less than to compromise the centerpiece of our defensive efforts in the war on terrorism."

The administration began making threatening noises like this as part of a clear campaign of intimidation. As the *Times* article detailed:

> [CIA Director Porter] Goss, speaking at a Senate intelligence committee hearing on Feb. 2, said: "It is my aim, and it is my hope that

we will witness a grand jury investigation with reporters present being asked to reveal who is leaking this information. I believe the safety of this nation and the people this country deserve nothing less."

Days later, on "The Laura Ingraham Show," a right-wing radio program, Dick Cheney remarked that he found Goss's threats "rather restrained." Consider the effects of these threats—from the highest levels of our government—on other people who may be tempted to come forward and expose other serious wrongdoing on the part of the administration. Could hearing that the Justice Department is "laying the groundwork for a grand jury inquiry that could lead to criminal charges" intimidate anyone who might consider blowing the whistle on other forms of serious misconduct by the Bush administration?

Whatever one's views are on the NSA scandal, disclosure by *The New York Times* of the warrantless eavesdropping program has accomplished exactly what newspapers are designed to achieve—namely, ensuring that highly controversial government programs, particularly ones of dubious legality, are subject to public debate and not concealed by the government. It has long been clear that the *Times* disclosed only that information necessary to enable such public discussion, but purposely withheld—and continues to withhold—all operational details of the eavesdropping program that could even remotely jeopardize national security.

This blatant use of the forces of criminal prosecution to threaten whistle-blowers and intimidate journalists is nothing more than the naked tactics of street thugs and authoritarian juntas. The United States has never imprisoned journalists for reporting on governmental wrongdoing, even when such disclosures entail classified information. America has always relied upon an aggressive and free press to scrutinize the government's conduct—especially conduct that the government seeks to conceal. That is why Thomas Jefferson long ago said, "If I had to choose between government without newspapers, and newspapers without government, I wouldn't hesitate to choose the latter." Jefferson also prophetically warned: "Our first object should therefore be, to leave open to him all the avenues of truth. The most effectual hitherto found, is freedom of the press. It is therefore, the first shut up by those who fear the investigation of their actions."

America's Choice

Most Americans have an instinctive, unstated pride—and even grati-tude—about being American, because we know that we live in a country that is unique in ensuring that our lives are free of tyranny and oppres-sion. And while our system of government has exhibited an extraordinary stability and resilience—remaining firmly in place through a civil war, two world wars, and all sorts of internal struggles and conflicts—there is no guarantee that it will last forever.

Although the founders erected safeguards as durable and thorough as they could devise, they recognized that those safeguards were not invul-nerable. They foresaw the danger that future leaders would seek to capi-talize on our fears and on threats from external enemies in order to seize absolute and unchecked powers. And while there are numerous checks against the seizure of such power—the courts, the Congress, the press—those institutions are also prone to failure or co-option.

Ultimately, people will get the government they deserve. And our sys-tem of government and the individual liberties it so brilliantly guarantees will endure only if Americans, who are the beneficiaries of those liberties, take a stand for them and are willing to defend them when they are under assault. That is what Benjamin Franklin meant when he said, in response to being asked what had been created at the Constitutional Convention: "A republic, if you can keep it." Representatives in Congress will stonewall investigations only until the American people demand that the truth be revealed. A president can insist on the right to break the nation's laws only as long as Americans permit that to continue.

We now have a president who is claiming the power to break our laws and to act without any checks of any kind from the Congress, the courts, or the citizens. He and his administration have said this repeatedly and expressly, and they are not just mouthing words; they have acted on them repeatedly. They have broken our laws and exercised against Amer-ican citizens precisely the powers our Constitution is designed, at its core, to prevent.

Whether we will become a country in which the president can exer-cise unlimited power—whether we will fundamentally change the type of nation we are—will be determined exclusively by whether we allow this behavior to continue. We have the ability to stop it at any time and to demand that those responsible be held accountable. We have the ability to insist on adherence to constitutional principles and limitations on presidential power, rather than allowing President Bush's radical departure from our core political values to continue and worsen. That is the choice which we, as Americans, face, and the ultimate resolution of this crisis will be determined solely by what we choose.

Epilogue

As this book was being completed, an explosive controversy emerged over the administration's purported plans to launch a military offensive against Iran, which is allegedly acquiring nuclear weapons. In an April 17, 2006, article in *The New Yorker*, Seymour Hersh reported that the administration "has increased clandestine activities inside Iran and intensified planning for a possible major air attack." If true, the question of how the United States decides—or rather, *who* decides—to launch a massive assault against Iran will have a lot to do with the theories discussed in this book.

If the prowar officials in the Bush administration convince the president that some sort of surgical strike, major military attack, or "decapitation" assault against Iran is necessary, will the administration seek any sort of congressional authorization or public support to engage in whatever war action it desires? Very doubtful.

As we have seen, there is simply no question that the administration believes that the president has the inherent power under Article II to order any military action that can be linked, however broadly or loosely, to a defense of the country against terrorism. One need only look to the September 25, 2001, Yoo memorandum, still the official position of the entire executive branch. That memorandum's concluding proclamation of generally unlimited presidential power was discussed earlier in this book, but the bulk of the memorandum is devoted to a discussion of the president's authority to order military force even in the absence of congressional authorization. Here are some of Yoo's preliminary decrees:

> Further, the President has the constitutional power not only to retaliate against any person, organization, or State suspected of involvement in terrorist attacks on the United States, but also against foreign States suspected of harboring or supporting such organizations. Finally, the President may deploy military force preemptively

against terrorist organizations or the States that harbor or support them, whether or not they can be linked to the specific terrorist incidents of September 11. . . .

We conclude that the Constitution vests the President with the plenary authority, as Commander in Chief and the sole organ of the Nation in its foreign relations, to use military force abroad— especially in response to grave national emergencies created by sudden, unforeseen attacks on the people and territory of the United States. . . .

These powers give the President broad constitutional authority to use military force in response to threats to the national security and foreign policy of the United States.

Citing theories first espoused by the Nixon administration, the Bush administration sees its powers as being tantamount to those exercised by Abraham Lincoln during the incomparable crisis of the Civil War. Hence:

The power of the President is at its zenith under the Constitution when the President is directing military operations of the armed forces, because the power of Commander in Chief is assigned solely to the President. It has long been the view of this Office that the Commander-in-Chief Clause is a substantive grant of authority to the President and that the scope of the President's authority to commit the armed forces to combat is very broad. . . .

The President's complete discretion in exercising the Commander-in-Chief power has also been recognized by the courts. In the Prize Cases, 67 U.S. (2 Black) 635, 670 (1862), for example, the Court explained that, whether the President "in fulfilling his duties as Commander in Chief" had met with a situation justifying treating the southern States as belligerents and instituting a blockade, was a question "to be decided by him" and which the Court could not question, but must leave to "the political department of the Government to which this power was entrusted."

And anyone who believes that congressional authorization is required just because the Constitution vests in Congress the authority to declare war is, according to the memorandum, very confused:

If the Framers had wanted to require congressional consent before the initiation of military hostilities, they knew how to write such provisions. . . .

Given this context, it is clear that Congress's power to declare war does not constrain the President's independent and plenary constitutional authority over the use of military force. . . .

The centralization of authority in the President alone is particularly crucial in matters of national defense, war, and foreign policy, where a unitary executive can evaluate threats, consider policy choices, and mobilize national resources with a speed and energy that is far superior to any other branch.

The memorandum goes on and on like that—touting "the centralization of authority in the President alone" in all matters relating to national security. That opinion is backed by a forty-two-page Department of Justice document issued in January 2006 that makes clear that it is the prevailing view within the executive branch.

As a nation, we can and should engage in vigorous debates over whether a military offensive against Iran is desirable, prudent, disastrous, or just plain crazy. But it is just as crucial that we realize that the Bush administration has embraced theories of executive power which assert that the president has the authority to initiate a military attack on Iran regardless of whether the American people, or their representatives in Congress, approve of such an attack. Congress could refuse to authorize this military offensive, or it could enact legislation banning it, but the president's view of his own powers means that he would still have the authority to launch an attack anyway. As the Iran debate proceeds, it is necessary to remember that the president believes he is the "sole organ" in all such matters, and he has full, limitless, and unchecked authority to do whatever he wants.

Under Article I, Section 8 of our Constitution, the founders assigned the right to declare war to the Congress, not the president. Whatever the merits of initiating an attack on Iran, under our system of government this preemptive war should not be launched without a vigorous public debate and congressional authorization. At the very least, Americans, based on these most fundamental constitutional principles, should be willing to resist the notion that the president's powers are unlimited and absolute when it comes to the question of whether this country will begin another war.

I will be following these and other developments relating to the constitutional issues discussed in this book on my blog, Unclaimed Territory (http://glenngreenwald.blogspot.com/). I invite you to join the conversation there, but more importantly, to push these issues of presidential power onto the agenda for public discussion. Ask your elected representatives about it, talk to your co-workers, friends, and family, contact the media, or start your own blog. Let your voice be heard.

Acknowledgments

This book was a collaborative effort on every level. Jennifer Nix, who is a true visionary in book publishing, conceived of the idea and single-handedly caused it to be published. The book's editor, Safir Ahmed, fulfills many more functions than a typical book editor, and virtually every aspect of the book has been shaped by him. Working Assets Publishing made a swift and impressive commitment to the book's objectives.

Many of the ideas and arguments in the book are drawn from discussions with the participants and contributors at my blog, Unclaimed Territory, who provide an ongoing source of thought-provoking analysis and collective wisdom on these issues every day. One day, I asked in passing on my blog if anyone would be interested in helping me with the research for this project, and within twenty-four hours, I received more than two hundred offers of help—from lawyers, physicians, professors, military professionals, students, homemakers, and retired people. Concern over the political crisis in our country is pervasive and intense, and the diversity, energy, and talent among people wanting to take a stand for our country are extraordinary and encouraging.

Most of the research for the book was done by four blog readers who volunteered: Bryce A. Pashler, an attorney in Manhattan; Dave Harris, a sophomore at Michigan State University and an assistant coach for Okemos High School's debate team; Gaelen Burns, president of an information technology and security company who, as he put it, "became politically active with the events of 9/11, and has fallen in love with our Constitution as a result"; and blogger Dave Johnson. Johns Hopkins University Professor Hilary Bok provided invaluable suggestions for improving the manuscript. And a special thanks to Mason Thomas for enabling me to get where I needed to go.

Finally, infinite and eternal thanks to Jason Buchtel and David Miranda Greenwald.

Glenn Greenwald is a constitutional lawyer and author of the political blog Unclaimed Territory, which he founded in 2005. After graduating from New York University's School of Law, Greenwald was a litigator at Wachtell, Lipton, Rosen & Katz in Manhattan, and then founded his own firm, Greenwald Christoph, with a focus on constitutional issues. His reporting and analysis have been cited in numerous political magazines and he appears frequently on television and radio news programs. His blog has become a much-cited source on issues of presidential power.

ABOUT THE PUBLISHER

Working Assets is a wireless, phone, credit card and publishing company that, through its services, generates donations to progressive causes. Since 1985, the company has donated over $50 million to organizations working for international freedom, equality, justice, alternative media, public education and the environment. To learn more about Working Assets services, go to WorkingAssets.com.